THE YANKEE
PEDDLERS
OF
EARLY
AMERICA

THE YANKEE
PEDDLERS
OF
EARLY
AMERICA

by

J. R. DOLAN

Clarkson N. Potter, Inc./Publisher, New York

*With deepfelt gratitude to
my son, Dick, and my daughter, Peggy,
for their practical help and moral support
in the preparation of this book.*

Contents

Acknowledgments

Illustrations

Page 17,   Eric Sloan's OUR VANISH-ING LANDSCAPE, Wilfred Funk, Inc.

Page 150 (top),   The Metropolitan Museum of Art, Gift of Mr. and Mrs. William A. Moore, 1923.

Page 150 (bottom),   The Metropolitan Museum of Art, Rogers Fund, 1928.

Page 158,   The Metropolitan Museum of Art, Kennedy Fund, 1918.

Page 159,   The Metropolitan Museum of Art, Bequest of William B. Whitney, 1937.

Page 162,   F. J. Britten's BRITTEN'S OLD CLOCKS AND WATCHES AND THEIR MAKERS, E. P. Dutton & Co., Inc.

Page 180,   Richard Carter Barret, Bennington, Vermont.

Page 181,   Mary Earle Gould's EARLY AMERICAN WOODEN-WARE, The Pond-Ekberg Co.

Page 240,   Brown Brothers.

Introduction

Daily life in early America has come to have an increasing fascination for us. History as everyday living, rather than as formal politics or diplomacy, captures our imagination and stimulates our interest far more than scholarly accounts of wars, treaties, or the making of laws; we like to know what our ancestors did each day, what they wore, how they lived, what they ate, what their amusements were, how America looked in the seventeenth and eighteenth centuries. We plan our vacations to visit historic sites; we go to see the reconstructed village of Salem, Illinois, to find out how the young Abe Lincoln lived. Old Sturbridge Village in Massachusetts shows us the New England of a century and a half ago; and Williamsburgh in Virginia, so faithfully and painstakingly rebuilt by the Rockefellers, shows us how our ancestors lived when we were still a Colonial people.

Local museums such as the Old Museum Village of Smith's Clove, New York, give us a splendid opportunity to study in detail the objects our ancestors made and used, and, indeed, the whole way of life they reflect. One of the most recent examples of this preservation of the past can be found in The Great Smoky Mountains National Park. The area is known as Cade's Cove, several square miles of woodsy mountain country, far from modern transportation, permanently segregated from progress so that coming generations may actually visit cabins typical of the mountain people a century ago.

We collect antiques, searching out old glass, clocks, pewterware, tinware, and furniture, not only because we have discovered that they are fine in design and craftsmanship, but also because we derive pleasure from these direct links to our near past. We like to have history recreated for us for our pleasure as well as for our information; and the purpose of this book is to show, through the story of the Yankee peddler, how civilization and culture made their way from the eastern seacoast cities via the peddlers to remote inland settlements and the isolated pioneers who farmed the wilderness.

The Yankee peddler has long been a picturesque and colorful figure; for too long we have thought of him as an idler and a vagrant who moved from one remote settlement to another because he lacked the brains or the enterprise to set up a stable business. In reality he was often a shrewd, ambitious, tough character whose dogged courage and keen imagination played a vital role in our social and economic development. It is hardly an exaggeration to say that our entire Middle West and South would have remained regions of thinly settled backwoodsmen far into the nineteenth century if the lowly peddler had not carried the materials of civilization to the people who lived there. The pioneer who, with his family, left the settled East to find a spot where he could start a new life was a poor man even by the standards of that day. Men of even modest wealth and position did not uproot themselves from the established ease of a seacoast city to strike out into the wilderness; such a move was left for the man with courage and ambition but a very small store of worldly goods.

Unless he could go westward by boat up one of the coastal rivers to find a homesite at its source, a settler had to cross the chain of mountains that runs from upper New York State almost to the Gulf. This meant he could carry with him only what he could put on a packhorse—if, indeed, he could afford that luxury.

Yet even before the pioneer had a roof on his cabin in what would later be Ohio, Indiana, Kentucky, or Tennessee, a peddler was likely to arrive at his door. In the 1700's the peddler would have an amazing assortment of little things in his trunk. We think of them as little things because in size they are, but if we measure them in terms of downright usefulness they become gigantic—needles and pins, buttons and combs, table knives and spoons—real necessities for a new settler. A few weeks later other peddlers would reach that cabin, no matter how isolated it was, with a somewhat different assortment. And if the settler had no cash (not an unusual condition), he could buy with beaver pelts or other items that the surrounding forest could be made to give up.

Thus, well before the pioneer had a chance to harvest even his first crop, he was trading the products of his labor for the things families must have if they are not to sink to a level of civilization we left behind many centuries before.

This meant that the peddlers themselves had to undertake arduous journeys into harsh wilderness and to know what to bring with them that would be of use to the families who lived there. Many times they had to travel almost without roads or trails, then make their way back to the cities bearing whatever they had exchanged for their goods. By the eighteenth century a whole network of such itinerant traders had come into existence and were forming the basis of commerce as we now know it.  Who were they? Where did they come from? How did they obtain their goods and sell them? How did they travel and what did they find along those lonely back trails? In the chapters that follow, we shall look at the Yankee peddler, at his place in the fabric of early American life, at the varied functions he performed, at the (sometimes) rambling and haphazard ways he followed before he became an established man of affairs and the colorful traveler of lost trails disappeared forever from the back roads and the highways of America.

PART I

THE PEDDLERS
TAKE TO THE ROAD

1

Boston: The Origin
of the Yankee Peddler

———————◆———————

Like baked beans on Saturday night and pie for breakfast, the Yankee peddler undoubtedly had his
origin in staid old Boston in the late seventeenth century; at least, the city fathers have never successfully
denied it. But as Boston was the chief port of the East
Coast and the best source of those manufactured goods
which could be carried through the town and over the
country trails, it was the most likely place for a peddler
to start his career. Early records do not show who the
first Yankee was who shouldered a bundle of goods and
began to knock on doors around the town, but he must
have done reasonably well because the whole area soon
blossomed out with imitators. Word of their doings and
new occupation must have reached as far as Plymouth
very quickly, because soon the old Baypath Trail that
connected the two settlements was dotted with peddlers,
and the trails to Salem and other nearby towns were
similarly thronged.

Thus a way of living was born that was to last for
nearly three centuries; it was a way that would have a
strong appeal for young men for generations to come,
that would make them the pipeline between sources of
supply in the East and the farthest-flung settlements
in the Middle West and South. The peddler alone was
to be the carrier of otherwise unavailable supplies to

Old print of Boston in 1700's.

pioneer families well into the nineteenth century. Retail stores in the modern sense of the word did not exist at all until about 1800, and then only in those places, few and far between, where transportation facilities made a general store possible.

Meanwhile Boston was the center of commerce, and since it was the birthplace of the Yankee peddler, we might well look at the town in the period between 1650 and the end of the century. It had a population then of about 10,000, and immigration from England in the latter part of this period came almost to a stop, not to be resumed in any strength for more than a century. By the late 1600's Boston had become a community of second- and third-generation Americans tied to the mother country by every bond of loyalty that blood and tradition could forge.

The town must have been drab-looking. Most of the

houses were small with only two or three rooms; they were made by driving small saplings into the ground and weaving these together with switches, and then plastering the whole thing, inside and out, with a mixture of clays and anything that resembled hair that the builder could get hold of. The roof was thatched, of course, and, with rare exceptions, the outside was unpainted. Here and there you could see one of the newer types of home, the kind we call the saltbox from its resemblance to that object. These were quite an improvement on the old plaster-and-sapling construction, frequently having clapboard sides and tiny diamond-shaped glazed windows. At least one brickyard was operating in Boston at this period, but its production was far too small to allow bricks to be used for anything but fireplaces and chimneys.

SALTBOX STYLE

The houses were not made of logs, though nineteenth century artists try to convince us they were. They loved to show quiet and peaceful scenes of the Pilgrim Fathers going to church always against a background of typical log cabins. As a matter of fact, not a log cabin existed in the entire Massachusetts Bay Colony and scarcely anywhere on the entire East Coast. The use of logs for building was brought in at a later period by the Swedes. To build a cabin out of logs a man had to go out to the nearest woods, select some thirty to forty sizable tress, chop them down, lop off all the branches, and then drag all the logs to his building site. At this stage he had merely delivered the raw materials for his house; he still had the entire job of building to do. The thrifty Yankees found it much easier and quicker to build the same type of home they had always known in the southwestern counties of England whence most of them had come.

The streets of Boston at that time meandered from here to yonder, somewhat in the pattern they follow to this day, except that no street was distinguished by a name and no house had a number. Every street was entirely unpaved, of course, and each was full of holes and hollows and dotted everywhere with tree stumps. What did it matter? One traveled around town on foot or on the back of a horse, and we can be sure that nobody complained because no other way had ever been heard of.

Runty-looking pigs rooted peacefully at will to be claimed in the fall by the owners, if the pigs had not died of disease or starvation and the owner was able to identify his own by the way he had earmarked them. The way Yankees treated their pigs, at that period of history, would make a modern Iowa farmer curl up and die of horror. The pig was expected to provide the owner with food—not the other way around.

About the only bits of color to be seen in the streets were the swinging signs of the inns. These inns or taverns were called "ordinaries" at this time, and the gaily painted signs in front of them carried pictures of ships or anchors or some object that would serve to identify the building as a place of refreshment for the tired citizen and a lodging for travelers or for sailors, because Boston was always full of sailors. A sign carried a picture as well as the name of the establishment because at that time relatively few of the population could read, and a picture was the simplest means of identification.

The arrival of a ship from England was by no means an uncommon occurrence, but it was always an exciting one for the simple reason that not much else happened in Boston. Every port in England was sending shiploads of both raw materials and finished goods to Boston, and as many as fifteen ships might be seen any day anchored in the bay or tied up at the pier. If your memory goes back even a little before the days when automobiles and trucks became common in our streets, especially if you lived in a small town, you can appreciate what the arrival of a ship meant to Bostonians because you can remember the excitement caused by the arrival of the daily or biweekly train in your town, when everyone who was not, for some unavoidable reason, tied to one particular spot would be drawn to the station to see who came in or who might be leaving: When the 3:35 from the city arrived at the station, with its bell ringing and black smoke puffing out of its stack, and the conductor swung off the step of the front coach with his watch in his hand, anything could happen—

perhaps a pretty girl or a handsome man would appear, or a drummer with a sample case.

Let us imagine the arrival of a ship in Boston as seen through the eyes of the town crier—we'll call him Orrin Willis. For all his sixty years he stands straight as a ramrod as he walks importantly along the street with his long telescope swinging by his side and a great brass handbell, muffled with a bit of cloth at the moment, hooked to his belt on the other side.

"Mornin' to ye, Captain. Will you be gettin' out today? The tide will turn about noon if you can make it."

Walking along, he notes that the *Primrose* is still tied up, but the noise and clatter of its crew indicates it will be under way by the turn of the tide.

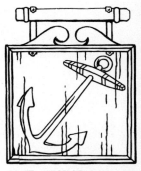

BLUE ANCHOR INN, 1682

"Wonder if she's got a full load of fish—she had only half a load yesterday and she may have had to take on some of that lumber. Well, I guess it will be all right, it'll be mighty welcome over there. I heard they don't hardly have wood enough over there to build a fire with nowadays, while we got plenty here."

Glancing over his shoulder toward what is now Tremont Street, to the Meetinghouse with the only publicly displayed clock in all Boston, he springs into action. Taking the muffle out of his bell, he unhooks it and begins ringing and calling out, "eleven by the clock and all is well." A moment or two of this, while he continues to pace northward toward the fishing piers, and he replaces the muffle, hangs the bell at his belt again, and resumes his stately walk. He pauses before the swinging sign of the Blue Anchor, rubs his chin reflectively for a moment, makes a decision and walks in. But he is hardly inside when he hears a shout from the street, a commotion that to his practiced ear can mean only the arrival of another ship, and down to the dock and out to the very end of the pier he goes, almost forgetting his dignity in the excitement of the arrival with its cargo of news and people and things from the homeland. He swings his great glass into action, aiming it far out into the bay, to exactly the same place that the great ships of today use when they come into Boston.

"Looks like the *Derby Dell*—Captain Ellers. Nope,

can't be, she doesn't have that rig. Might be the *Manchester* with Captain Withers, but she ain't due for a couple of weeks more—I do wish they would think of me when they puts the names on these ships. They always put the name on the stern so you can't see it till they almost get clear into the dock. How am I going to let the people know what ship has come in unless I can see her name?"

She is still a half-mile away from the pier with all her sails furled tightly, and her two great yawls, each manned by six men, are warping her into the dockside before Orrin can make out her name, the *Amorancy,* from Liverpool. Hoisting one foot to the top of a low-driven pile, the town crier waits to greet her master, Captain Ezra, before setting out on his swing through the town to announce the arrival. He is thinking, perhaps, "Hope she ain't loaded with furniture this time. Last time that's all she was carryin' and they ain't all sold yet—too dang expensive. You can get tables and things right here just as good and a lot cheaper."

As Orrin Willis spreads the news of the ship's arrival, a milling crowd gathers on the pier; and in due time Orrin himself comes down to find out what the ship is carrying. Some of the throng are moved merely by curiosity; others have a more practical reason for being there; for instance, one of Orrin's duties is to find out what the cargo is and to inform the local importers and wholesalers. It may be large rolls of textiles, crates of pewter, paper, or window glass. But being sharp-eyed and experienced, Orrin knows that, in all likelihood, every member of the crew has brought in a quantity of small items that he bought back in England for private speculation. A sailor can pack a lot of needles, pins, buttons, combs, spools of thread, and spoons and knives for the table into a small bundle. (Forks were not yet generally used.) In Boston and in outlying settlements there was a ready market for such items, which were constantly wearing out or getting lost and had to be replaced.

A good-sized ship such as this might carry 102 persons; it had a displacement of 180 tons, about the size of a modern tugboat. Many of the persons aboard were

passengers; but let us suppose that 25 of them were members of the crew. These men would find on the dock 25 eager young Bostonians who were only too willing to acquire—by whatever means of payment they could—the small merchandise that the sailors brought; they could easily dispose of it around the town. Today we would call this procedure smuggling, but at that time it had no particular name; it was an accepted business practice. There was no system to business; it was governed (with the exception of the liquor and tavern business) neither by law nor custom. Every man operated on his own; he could buy anything from anyone willing to sell it, and sell it to anyone who wanted to buy, and only price was the subject of bargaining. This was the rule throughout the civilized world. And so our twenty-five young men haggled over the contents of the sailors' packs. This, as far as we know, was the origin of the Yankee peddler.

As the crowds on the piers thin out and the sailors go off to find food and drink after six to ten weeks of a salt pork and fish diet in cramped quarters, Orrin Willis goes back up the street to give news of the heavier cargo that has arrived on the ship.

Stopping at the big house of Amos Amesbury, he knocks with the big brass knocker, thinking, perhaps, "This Mr. Amesbury's made a mint of money by sellin'—doesn't have to go out himself any more—he just buys the goods wholesale and sells them to them that does"—meaning, of course, the itinerant peddlers who plied the roads.

Mr. Amesbury has indeed done well; he was once a peddler himself in the Boston area, buying items from ships' crews as they came in. Now he has become an importer and wholesaler—he buys any and all items that came into Boston, even whole shiploads, and sells them to anyone who is interested in reselling them to the consumer.

In fact, Boston at this time had several men in Mr. Amesbury's position, men who had graduated from peddler to importer. Edward Ward, an Englishman who spent some time over here, has left us a fairly accurate description of the city, dated 1699, in which he said: "In the chief, or high street, there are stately edifices some of which must have cost the owners two and three thousand pounds . . . for the fathers of these men were Tinkers and Peddlers." A tinker, at that time, was a man who peddled services instead of goods. He was particularly skilled in repairing pewter and went from house to house looking for cracked or bent pewterware. He was probably the first of the service peddlers, men who were to become also as numerous as those who sold goods.

Orrin Willis delivers to Mr. Amesbury, or one of his employees, news of the cargo that has arrived—the official cargo, not the small bundles traded by sailors to the young men who are, if they are shrewd and lucky, the future Mr. Amesburys.

Having delivered his news, Orrin Willis goes back to his normal routine as town crier; the young men with their newly acquired pins, buttons, or spoons, are off to peddle them; and the sailors in all probability go to an inn. Boston at this period was always full of sailors, and inns and taverns may be presumed to have done a thriving business, to judge from the records of the laws that governed them. Nowadays ships unload as fast as they can and turn around for the homeward journey; but at a time when it took many weeks to cross the Atlantic the crew was allowed a liberal period of time ashore, from a week to three weeks, before boarding for another long dry spell. So there were always a couple of hundred sailors in town and the inns did a thriving business.

Not that their trade was restricted to travelers. We know from the strict regulations of taverns that sold ale, beer, wine, cider, and later rum from the West Indies, that local residents accounted for most of their steady trade.

Getting a license to run an inn at this time was not too easy; the straitlaced fathers of the community realized that an inn could become a "den of iniquity" if it got into the control of the wrong people, and they seem to have done their best to limit licenses to citizens of good standing. You might be a selectman, a tax assessor, or even a member of the Common Council, and still

lose your license if you were reported in violation of any of a long list of petty charges. But regardless of your political standing in the community you had to be a member of the reigning church. Boston at that time was a tight combination of Church and State with no toleration whatever for believers in anything else.

One of the regulations concerning taverns that seems very strange to us was the insistence on at least one tavern being near each church—yes, *near* each church —quite the opposite of our commonly accepted laws which insist on a specified distance between the two. Church services at that time went into many hours of continuous session, and it just might be that those old Yankees were as practical about this sort of thing as they were about everything else, such as making it invitingly easy for a man to have a couple of nice hot drinks just before entering church, to keep out the chill during the long sermon, and a couple more when the service was over.

Another example of their practical minds might be seen in their regulations on the amount of beer one customer was allowed to buy in one day. The rule was that the innkeeper could sell one quart only *between* meals to a man, but *with* a meal he could sell him as many as he cared for. Let us see how that could add up. Since coffee was still almost unknown in the colonies, let us assume that our man has a quart of beer with his ham and eggs in the morning. At ten o'clock he would have another quart in lieu of our modern coffee break. Then at lunch he might manage two quarts, and sometime in the middle of the afternoon he could have his between-meals quart and linger over this until time for an early dinner. So, along with his codfish, broiled over the open fire, he could absorb two more quarts easily enough, and when he felt it was time to call it a day he was entitled to another. They don't seem to have called this last one "one for the road," but nevertheless it was just that. Imagine what capacity the Yankees must have had if such limitations were considered necessary.

To offset this, however, they had strict regulations against idleness. A man could be whipped on the bare back clear to the border of the township, picked up there by another official and whipped to the border of that one—all for merely being caught spending more than one hour in a tavern during working hours. How did this work out in practice? The idea evidently was to chase the loafer out of the township. If he could run a bit faster than the official he might never feel the bite of the whip at all since he could pace himself just ahead of the lash. It is unlikely that any law against idleness was enforced against sailors; and as for our young peddlers, they were on the move enough of the time so that the law did not often catch up with them.

From a young peddler of spools and buttons to a merchant prince like Amos Amesbury the importer was a long road, and it might take several generations to travel it—if one even got that far. Behind the difficulties of the Boston peddler and merchant lay the incredibly shortsighted trade policies of the mother country, which were to continue until the end of the colonies' second war with England in 1815.

One basic restriction was that no manufacturing should be done in the colonies. A man might make a spinning wheel for his wife, if he had the skill, but he could not make one to sell to his neighbor; the neighbor would have to buy one imported from England.

Another rule was that any goods that England might "buy" from us, such as beaver pelts or other furs, dried fish, or lumber, must be paid for with English goods. The theory was that the colonies existed solely for the benefit and prosperity of Englishmen back home, and no consideration was shown for those Englishmen who had left for the New World to improve their fortunes. A consequence of this policy of trading only in goods was a shortage of currency, and what a problem it must have been, not only to the peddlers, but to anyone who engaged in business. No English money was allowed to go to the colonies; the colonists had to take payment in English-made furniture or other manufactured goods. In spite of every effort to forbid the importation of English currency, however, a considerable volume of sterling was in circulation, though not nearly enough to take care of normal business, even with prices as low as they were.

For example, the prices the people of Boston paid for food would make a modern housewife green with envy—unless she examined closely the wage scale of that day. A housewife could go down to the pier where the fishing fleet came in and buy a ten-pound codfish for twopence—not per pound, but the entire fish. But her hardworking breadwinner had to be a skilled workman and put in a ten- or twelve-hour day merely to earn two shillings. Meat and poultry were correspondingly low in price; a twenty-pound turkey might be had for two shillings. But except when nature provided it in winter there was no such thing as refrigeration, so not much was to be gained through such bargains if 90 per cent of the food went bad before it could be eaten.

And in view of the scarcity of currency, what could be used to buy the necessities of daily life? Many small commodities had to serve as cash, one of them being musket balls, made of lead and worth a farthing each. However you could not pay a very large grocery bill with a keg of bullets, as you were not allowed to pass more than a dozen bullets at a time to any one person.

The cash shortage was alleviated somewhat by the use of Spanish money. Trade with the West Indies was heavy, and Spanish doubloons and silver coins were always showing up.

But this only complicated small commercial transactions, and to simplify matters the General Court of Massachusetts in 1652 decided to set up its own mint and to coin what was called the Pine Tree shilling. Old records indicate that this step pleased the Bostonians of the time, but it is doubtful that it brought about any real improvement. Certainly a merchant would not refuse gold or silver for his goods, regardless of where the coins originated; so his cash drawer would now have three systems of currency instead of two, and no such thing as a bank existed to change currency or offer credit on a uniform basis. When it came to money-

Early American Currency: silver Pine Tree Shillings. *The Metropolitan Museum of Art, Bequest of A. T. Clearwater, 1933.*

lending, any individual could set himself up as a bank and lend money to anyone at whatever rate of interest he could get, or borrow from others, at interest, if he wanted to extend his operations beyond his cash at hand; there was no supervision by government, and the private bankers did nothing to regularize the currency situation.

But at least the Pine Tree shilling was a step toward a uniform legal currency. The General Court appointed one John Hull, whose daughter was married to a Boston judge named Sewall, actually to make the shillings. The court gave him a contract which was to run from 1652 to 1686 and undertook to supply him with the silver he would need to mint the coins; for his labor he was to receive fifteen pence for every twenty shillings he turned out. This figures out at about 6 per cent, and since the contract had about thirty-five years to run, John Hull must have felt pretty good about it. We can guess that he did, because the court made several efforts to buy back the contract or at least to get Mr. Hull to lower the rate. But not Mr. Hull; he had a good thing going and he had no intention of changing it. He lived to a ripe old age with never a worry about unemployment or the cost of living. One indication of his economic position was the fact that he gave his daughter, on the occasion of her marriage to John Sewall, a wedding gift of her weight in Pine Tree shillings. These facts are given us in the diary the learned judge left; but he omitted one detail about the wedding gift: was Miss Hull a calorie-counter or did she let nature take its course in adding to her weight?

With England's severe trade policies and the confused currency situation, a young man had a hard time getting a start in business. In addition, the social distinctions in the theocratic state were rigid, the privilege of voting was limited, and most men had no voice in the conduct of public affairs nor any chance to improve their condition.

You were a "freeman" if you owned property worth at least two hundred pounds, and were a member of the church. With this distinction went the privilege not only of voting but of wearing better clothes and being called "mister."

However, if your worldly goods totaled something less than two hundred pounds, you not only had no voice in the conduct of public affairs, but you went by the title of "goodman," and your wife would be "goodwife," or plain "goody" to her friends. In the late 1600's, some 80 per cent of the population belonged to this non-voting class.

A boy was expected to go to school until he was about fourteen, regardless of the status of his parents. But then he was expected to make some kind of decision as to his future, just as a youth of today is, although now the decision is made at a later age. If his father belonged to the small wealthy upper class, he had some choice; he could continue his education (possibly in England) or go into the family business. Or he could go into the ministry; every family of any consequence was expected to contribute at least one son to the church. If he wanted to become a doctor, a young fellow could "read medicine" with a practicing physician; and if he had ambitions to follow the law he made a similar arrangement with a lawyer. He could become an innkeeper if he could meet the fairly stiff requirements of that profession which was probably a good deal more respected then than it is today.

But if he belonged to the lower orders the choices were less appealing and offered less chance for advancement. He could follow the sea as a sailor, of course, with the certainty of adventure and the remote possibility of some day becoming master of his own ship. He could join the crew of one of the numerous fishing boats with the hope of laying the foundations of a codfish fortune, and many young men tried it. Shipbuilding offered great opportunities in the Boston area; it was a thriving business since lumber was more plentiful here than in England. "Ships were built of wood and men were built of iron."

A young man could apprentice himself to any of several trades, such as tailor, candlemaker, soap-boiler, or silversmith, and after serving about seven years without pay he could open his own shop.

Such a restricted society was, of course, bound to produce resistance. Thomas Hooker, a Puritan minister who had never been satisfied with the religious test for voting, had led a group of over a hundred settlers west to the Connecticut River and south to what is now Hartford. More people followed into the comparatively lush Connecticut River Valley, founding Windsor and Wethersfield and Saybrook. Roger Williams, in the same year Hooker departed—1639—packed his bag in Salem and made a midnight run to the south, where he bought a sizable parcel of real estate which he called Providence. He had no use for the Puritan idea of Church and State being one, and he attracted many people of similar views as Providence and other new towns nearby drew hundreds of new home-seekers.

These new towns provided virgin territory for the profession of peddler. Aside from following the sea it was the only occupation that offered possibilities of adventure; and then, as now, young men wanted to explore new and strange places, to seek excitement, and to travel. The hometown market of Boston was pretty well glutted with peddlers, and young men who chose that occupation began to cast an eye on the newer settlements as possible markets. Finding himself in possession of a bundle of notions such as needles and pins and buttons, a young man would set out on the trails south or west of Boston, where he knew he would find people in need of his wares.

And so, as the seventeenth century drew to a close, we find young men from every established settlement taking to the trail, either on foot with packs on their backs, or on horseback with saddlebags full of merchandise. Surely not one of them ever thought of himself as a member of a large commercial army that was to grow to gigantic size in the century ahead and to become a vital factor in the building of the nation and its business.

2

How Peddlers Traveled: From Indian Trail to Modern Expressway

In the America of the early 1700's when New England's peddlers began to fan out into the Middle West and South with a pack full of notions, nothing but an all-consuming desire for financial profit or an overwhelming thirst for adventure could possibly have made them suffer the tortures of travel by land at a time when nothing we could call a road even existed. Only the most primitive kind of animal and Indian trail, sometimes barely perceptible to the untrained eye of a town-bred New England boy, linked one settlement with another, and the hardships of traversing these dim pathways were incredible.

Today we are accustomed to smooth ribbons of concrete that lead us to virtually any part of the country we want to reach; and we are aggrieved when a highway turns out to be a mere two-lane affair. We can average fifty miles an hour all day long; five hundred miles between breakfast and dinner is not uncommon. We cross rivers and streams without even slowing down to notice their names.

But for a full three centuries of our life as a nation the very best roads in the country were so poor that they would not even be shown on a modern road map. Even an "unimproved" road on a modern map slows us down to forty miles an hour. In the 1700's map-makers would have exhausted the language trying to find a term for the very best roads of the times. There was hardly anything you could even walk along; traveling for pleasure was unheard of, and the Yankee peddler's most onerous task was merely getting to some place where he could sell his wares. Yet without him our road system would have lagged far behind its actual development; the peddlers built the roads—not in the literal sense, but in the sense that their need and their constant demand for them spurred road-building.

Until modern times the only people who ever really built roads were the Romans—built them, that is, by surveying the terrain between the points they wished to connect by road, determining the shortest distance, avoiding water as much as possible, and keeping to level ground as much as they could. Once these preliminaries were finished, then the stonemasons went to work. Labor in unlimited quantities must have been available; they hauled huge boulders from wherever they could find them to the right-of-way, lined them up along the course, using the larger ones in the hollows and the smaller ones on the higher ground to cut down the grades. And when all this foundation was built these sturdy Romans, or their slaves and enemy captives, set to work crushing large stones into small pieces and loading them into baskets to be poured into the crevices of the roadbed and strewn evenly over the surface. The quality of roads built that way gave such lasting results that many of them are in use today with no repair other than resurfacing at intervals.

But the old Romans never reached our shores. With the passing of that race the whole idea of actually building permanent and preplanned roads seems to have died out completely. From the fourth century on through the Middle Ages and into the nineteenth century not a single road in this country or any other was designed and built, in an engineering sense, and certainly not with the old Roman technique. Any roads that existed here in the early part of the eighteenth century "just grew."

Undoubtedly the very first roads in this country were the paths worn by the feet of wild animals in their daily search for food. Countless thousands of deer lived in our forests but the trouble with the paths they made was that they never seemed to go any place that human beings could find useful. The deer likes to bed down at night on the top of a knoll where he can keep his nose into the wind to detect the approach of an enemy and in the early morning take off for his feeding area near a marsh or river seldom more than a mile or two from where he spent the night. These deer paths are a fairly common sight in many parts of the country even today, but because of their lack of purposeful direction they have never been much help to our road-builders.

On the other hand, in later years, the buffalo were in some cases a very real help. They were huge creatures weighing well over half a ton, and great droves of them used to travel long distances in their search for food, water, and a salt lick. It is easy to imagine what a trail a few hundred of these big animals would make through almost any kind of cover: they would trample and knock down every bit of vegetation except the larger trees and their instincts would guide them to the fords in the great rivers. The paths they would leave through the wilderness would be as wide as our finest expressway and probably just about as well surveyed too; but of course they would not be very smooth. However, the American buffalo never seem to have traveled eastward in any large numbers, although traces of them have been found as far east as the mountains of western Pennsylvania. So as a help to our early pioneers seeking a path from the seaboard settlements into the Midwest they have to be counted out.

This leaves the Indian as the only living creature who might have inadvertently given the white man some help in his transportation problems. After all, the Indian was a human being; he walked on two feet, he stood erect, and he even lived in villages. Here and there the white men could see the paths the Indians had made through the forest and they reasoned that a path made by any human must go somewhere, otherwise why make it? So the early settlers all along our East Coast were constantly venturing gingerly along these trails farther and farther into the wilderness, frequently discovering that a trail actually did lead to some desirable spot such as a pleasantly situated site of some long-abandoned Indian village at the fork of a river.

To the lover of early American things in general these old Indian trails are of extraordinary interest. With the probable exception of the remains left by the Mound Builders they may be the most ancient man-made things in this country. The typical trail measured only eighteen to twenty inches wide; it seemed to wander aimlessly from place to place without rhyme or reason; but if you followed it long enough it would begin to make sense to you. You would note that when it came to a stream it might turn abruptly either up-stream or down for some distance until it came to the mouth of another stream emptying into it and forming the inevitable sand bar; and you realized that the Indian who first broke that path was no fonder of wet feet than you; he was simply looking for a ford where he could cross with the minimum of wading.

The Indian of course had no knowledge whatever of the wheel in even its simplest form when the first white men arrived. He also had no horses or any other kind of pack animal; he carried his worldly goods on his back, or more accurately on the back of his squaw, who trailed along in back of the brave, who was content to carry only his weapons. The absence of wheels, of course, accounted for the narrowness of the trail and in turn the narrowness accounted for the custom of walking in single file.

Following the trail, you ford the stream at the sand bar, where the water is so shallow that you hardly wet your feet, and you are faced with a long ridge running roughly parallel to the stream and maybe thirty to forty feet above its level. The slope is an easy one that you could climb in a moment, but no; the trail wanders along the base of the ridge, rising so gradually as to be almost imperceptible, until you are surprised sud-denly to find yourself on top of the ridge. You pause and look back to the spot where you first came to the base of the ridge and felt that you could climb it easily. It is fully a quarter of a mile back and you must have lost ten minutes or more in getting to the top of this ridge by the leisurely route chosen by some dusky savage who, ages ago, not only had the desire to go over this ridge, but decided how he would accomplish it. Countless descendants of that man apparently were quite content literally to follow in his footsteps, and the early white settlers had no other choice.

Here and there about the country, in the East and Middle West, traces of these old trails may still be found if you have the patience and the knowledge to know where to look for them. Where the ground is usually moist all year except during winter the trails were frequently so worn and packed down by plodding feet that they are many inches below the surrounding level. Sometime, when you are in the mood for it and also in a likely place, which will be roughly parallel to a modern highway, take a stick and poke carefully through the undergrowth, walking at right angles to the highway on either side of it. If you are lucky you may find a long narrow depression, not many steps from the road, beaten down by the moccasined feet of a hundred generations of the redman. If the season happens to be autumn, and the blue haze of that lovely season hangs in the air, you may be able still to "see" a long line of Indians walking solemnly along that path and trailing over the brow of the hill into the setting sun, their ghostly, moccasined feet as silent as they were long before even the Romans built their wondrous roads.

Of course it will seldom, if ever, be possible to follow such an old pathway for any distance; much of it will have been obliterated by some modern improvement, but if you could you might be genuinely surprised to find that it would lead you to the very same area that the modern road alongside it does—a ford in the river or maybe the confluence of two rivers where some proud city now stands and boastfully tells the world about the advantages of its location.

Although the eastern Indians usually lived in villages that might have a population of several hundred they never built anything of a permanent nature. Recent excavations on the sites of several Indian villages

in the East have brought to light many successive
layers of charred bones, broken clam shells, and other
remains proving that that site had been occupied and
reoccupied many, many times in the course of the centuries. The frequent movements of the Indians produced the trails that were to become the roads of the
white man in later years—a prime example being part
of the Boston Post Road skirting the north shore of
Long Island Sound; this undoubtedly was originally
an old trail of the warlike Pequots. Of course all of the
trails were not main arteries by any means; leading out
from a village might be one or two leading only short
distances to favorite hunting or fishing areas. The Indian was not inclined to maintain cordial relations with
members of another tribe, although there were exceptional cases where this happened; but the more common case was the trail connecting two unfriendly tribes
—this was the "war path," never used for other purposes.

Rivers and lakes were roads too; all the traveler had
to do was to find a way of crossing them or skirting
their shores. I was reminded of this a few years ago
when I first visited Mackinac, where Lake Michigan
joins Lake Huron. I knew Mackinac had been the
great fur-trading post of that area for many years, and
so I assumed that it was easily accessible. When I arrived at St. Ignace, however, and was told that this
was the end of the road, I was dumfounded. We were
told we would have to leave our car there and take a
boat. Accessible? How could an island in the strait be
accessible? Actually, if there are no roads, and you have
some kind of navigable craft, an island is the most accessible place there is. All you need is a boat or raft.
And, as we shall see, the Yankee peddlers, as they made
their way inland from the seacoast, availed themselves
of the innumerable waterways that would take them to
remote settlements.

Coastal rivers were roads too. A map of our East
Coast in the early to middle 1700's shows clearly that
early arrivals on the coast usually chose sites for their
homes at the mouth of a river where it flowed into the
ocean. This was natural, as a coastal river usually man-

On the Boston Post Road from New York, Postmaster General Benjamin Franklin, accompanied by his daughter, made an inspection tour.

aged to produce a protected harbor, and an active shipping trade with the mother country and the rest of the world was in almost immediate prospect. It is a bit harder to understand however why some early arrivals, instead of settling down in the coastal settlement to a routine that would allow their modern descendants to point with pride to them, almost immediately took to the water again. The temptation to paddle a canoe or pole a raft up one of the broad rivers into the interior must have been overpowering to many, because we find dozens of settlements far up these rivers founded hardly a generation after the city at the mouth of the river was settled. One of the factors that tempted them may have been the obvious ease of paddling up a gently flowing river winding pleasantly into a forest of giant trees in an unknown and mysterious interior. Another factor in their decision could have been the vastly greater difficulty presented by the trails through the forest. And, if the trip upriver proved disappointing, one could drift downriver with even greater ease. At any rate, by the time of the Revolution we find each of the coastal rivers had from one or two to as many as half a dozen fairly prosperous communities along its banks. As they cleared the land for farming they floated the great logs down the river to the town at its mouth where they were in demand for shipbuilding and for houses for the stream of still newer arrivals from Europe.

Since the animal and Indian trails were slow to develop into roadways the ingenious Yankee peddler took as many shortcuts as he could. He took to the water, and in doing so he was probably responsible for the birth of that now defunct institution that many of us still remember as the general store.

Settlements upriver were more accessible to peddlers than remote places that could be reached only by trail, and soon a thriving river commerce sprang up. When a canoe became too small to carry the goods the peddler acquired he bought himself a raft, which he poled upstream and floated back when he had disposed of his goods. Sometimes a small mast and a bit of sail would help him make the journey upstream. In any case, it was one way of getting a considerable supply of goods inland. It is probable that these raftloads of assorted merchandise gave birth to the general store as the upriver settlements became little towns. It is easy to imagine how it might have come into being and developed into the first retail store known to the backwoods settlers.

A young man would move his family up river to one of the new settlements, build a cabin for them on some nice bottom land, and begin clearing it for farming. Clearing land for planting is a difficult operation even today, in spite of all of our power-driven machinery, but even with the best tools available in the 1700's it must have been almost unbelievably hard work. Pick and shovel, ax and saw from sunup to sunset; and at the close of a day a man might have cleared only enough land for a tiny kitchen garden and would have to look forward to many weeks of such labor before he could even think of his place as a farm. Toward sunset one day a raft might tie up at his post on the river

37

bank. The peddler on it would toot his horn to attract the farmer and his family down to his raft to inspect his goods and buy a few things.

Perhaps that day the farmer had met with more than usual discouragement in his land-clearing operation and his mind started to slip back to his boyhood across the sea where his father had owned a small shop in which he sold such goods as he was able to get. He remembered that his father put in long days in his little shop, but it was also the family home so he was able to carry on the work of maintaining the home and take care of the shop at the same time; and our settler could never remember a day that the family did not have enough to eat. Why not a similar operation here? Why not see if he could buy the whole raft of goods from the peddler, put them in the front room of his cabin and sell them piece by piece to his neighbors? Let us see what there is on that raft. Beside the usual needles and pins, buttons and thread, some knives and spoons and pewter plates, and a small barrel of rum from the West Indies, a few pounds of tea and a couple of good English axes, a keg of powder—enough to start with. It probably took some bargaining to get it, as the peddler had counted on stopping at all the farms on the river banks and then putting a bundle of goods on his back and walking inland to other farms until he was sold out before going downriver for another load. But to sell the entire raft of goods at once, even at a great sacrifice, would mean that he could promptly return to the seaport, get another load and by the time he could get back the newly established merchant might be ready for more goods.

While no one can be sure now in which of the many river towns this operation first took place, there seems no doubt about its being the origin of the general store. Until well into the nineteenth century such stores were rather strictly confined to the river towns near the coast because of their relatively easy access to a seaport where they could buy "a whole raft of goods"—an expression we still use.

However, with such vast inland areas inviting settlement rivers alone could not be depended on for transportation, and it became imperative to find ways through the forests and wilderness by land. Gradually the old Indian trails became a little wider, trodden by leather boots and by horses' hooves. It was the Spaniards who first introduced the horse to this continent in the 1500's—but that was in the Southwest and none of them ever reached the northeastern states. But as early as 1635 a whole shipload of Flemish horses arrived in New England and proved so useful that more and more were imported. They were called Narragansett pacers, and were better adapted to the saddle than to pulling a vehicle. In fact, there were hardly any vehicles to pull and no roads to accommodate them.

No one ever traveled ten miles from home without making preparations to stay at least overnight, and even this distance was quite a journey. Indeed, there was little reason for anyone to go to the next town. Up to the time of the Revolution the settlements of New England were incredibly provincial. One indication of this is the fact that in the late 1700's Connecticut had well over two thousand cemeteries. You begin to realize what this means when you learn that at that time the whole state had less than fifty communities. Of course, one of the answers is that nearly every farm had its own private burial ground, a little plot off in the corner of the property where it would not get in the way of the work of the farm and where it would be handy to lay away each generation as it passed to its reward. Of course some communities maintained a public burying ground: it might be in the yard of the village meetinghouse or even in a corner of the village green. A story is told about one of these. The town selectmen were meeting to decide on building a fence around the burial ground. One of them took the floor to say "I ben't fur it, the folks in there can't git out and nobody outside of there wants to get in so what do we need a fence fur?"

It has been argued that the reason so many of the old farms in the East maintained a private burial ground stemmed from the custom in England whereby a portion of an estate was set apart for this purpose; and undoubtedly this does explain some of them. But these Yankees were usually more practical than sentimental, and I find it easier to believe that, faced with carrying a coffin a mile or two over the roads of that period, it was a lot more sensible to bury the body right on the farm.

However, the peak of provincialism seems to have passed with the Revolution. Like every war, even those in our own time, it forced large numbers of young men to leave family and friends and familiar places to meet men of widely different racial backgrounds and customs. When they returned to their homes nothing looked quite the way it used to. They had tasted the delights of seeing strange places and meeting new people, of being free from the restrictions of home, and wanted more of it.

Up to the close of the Revolution peddling had been looked upon as a workaday, humdrum business by the great majority of the young men of the colonies who had not tried it. There was scarcely a town of any size that did not have one or two young fellows earning a living that way. But with the return of the soldiers to the hometown the business of peddling suddenly took on a whole new appeal. Instead of settling down into the old rut of working on the family farm or learning a trade, here was a way that offered high adventure, a chance to go places and see things, of possible romance, of being one's own boss and earning a living at the same time.

In the fifteen years between the close of the war and the opening of the nineteenth century the number of peddlers on the roads doubled and trebled. From a tiny stream they grew into a torrent that would increase in volume and in social and economic importance for fully a century. Athirst for adventure, freed from the trade restrictions imposed on the colonies by England, the young peddlers broke loose from the narrow provincialism of the colonies, and one of the most important things they did was to get roads built. And as the number of roads increased more peddlers traveled them. A continuous chorus of voices demanding more roads brought them into existence. Indian trails would no longer suffice; pathways would not accommodate wagons, and now the peddler was beginning to think in terms of wagonloads instead of packloads. His loud and persistent clamor got him the roads and the wagons too.

The lawmakers in Virginia began building the first turnpike in this country in 1785. It ran from Alexandria (supposed at that time to be a coming metropolis) down into the lower Shenandoah Valley. No less a person than Thomas Jefferson was at least a moral backer of this daring venture and many think he had a financial stake in it too.

The Grand Jury of Baltimore caught the fever of road-building in 1787 and built a fairly good road complete with tollhouses from Baltimore out through Frederick, Reistertown, and all the way to York. Philadelphia built the Lancaster Turnpike and almost

The first extensive gravel surface road was the Philadelphia-Lancaster Turnpike built in 1795.

overnight the contagion of turnpike-building traveled up and down the coast and even inland for some distance. The turnpike with its picturesque tollhouse soon became a common sight all over the East. In some cases the local governments built new roads, but more frequently private corporations were set up for the purpose, and a profit of 20 per cent was not at all uncommon. The privilege of charging a toll for the use of a road implies that that road is superior to others, but the records indicate that frequently the only thing new about a toll road was the tollhouse.

However, by no means were all the roads poorly built; here and there some appeared that actually were superior. Gravel roads, for example, were fine for a short time. Gravel was abundant everywhere, but it was soon found that the iron tires of heavy wagons soon

A tollhouse on the Old Newburg Toll Road, New York. *New York Public Library.*

ground it into dust that blew away in the course of a couple of years.

Some road-builders, whose names have not come down to us, in Pennsylvania and at the very same time in Massachusetts, hit upon a big improvement over gravel. They broke stone into small pieces, making sure that no piece weighed more than a very few ounces, and spread them evenly over a crowned surface, un-mixed with soil, clay, or even sand, and found this produced a first-class roadway that lasted for years with a little resurfacing now and then. For some reason that I have never been able to account for, roads by this process came to be called "macadamized," al-though the facts seem to prove that these roads were built in several different localities before Loudon McAdam ever came to this country. McAdam did build this type of road in England and Scotland but not until several years after he had visited our shores and presumably had seen it here.

Today we are so accustomed to following a definite, named route when we set out on a trip of even as little as a hundred miles that we may not realize how very modern the whole idea of a named and marked route really is. We take Route 66 from Chicago all the way to the West Coast. In Maine we can start on Route 1 and stay on it all the way to Key West, Florida, or we can cross the entire continent without ever getting off Route 40. Needless to say these modern routes rep-resent largely the mere joining together of a great many short pieces of roadway and indicating their continuity by a common name and route number. Such an idea was undreamed of in the eighteenth century, of course, and largely because nobody ever dreamed of traveling overland even a small fraction of such a distance.

In 1789, when the ink on our Constitution had hardly had time to dry, our first road map appeared. Its creator was Christopher P. Colles, an Irish engineer who had come over shortly before the Revolution and had served under Washington during the entire war. Like every innovator Colles had dreams, dreams that told him that this young and vigorous nation was going to need road maps to guide the traveler. And he set to work to provide them, using some of the surveys he had made while in the army and new studies he made for the purpose. He clearly had in mind the necessity of frequent revisions as they became necessary but that time never arrived while he lived. Nobody would buy his road maps; nobody had the slightest reason to buy them. If a businessman living in any one of the large eastern cities in the seventeen eighties and nineties had to go to one of the other cities (and the need would have to be very urgent) he took a boat or if that failed he got on a horse and went there by the only road that existed. Colles deserved much better for his efforts but he was generations ahead of his time.

And so the peddler used the roads which everyone

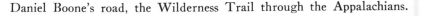

Daniel Boone's road, the Wilderness Trail through the Appalachians.

knew until he had to forge his own trails further west and south and the demand for a real road caused one to be built. There were many interruptions in the progress of road-building in America; when railroads became popular road-building ceased for a time. Yet the peddler's demand always lay behind the development of transportation, and our great modern network of expressways had its origin in the primitive trails the peddler trod.

During all of the latter half of the eighteenth century attempts were being made to pierce the Appalachian mountain range that separated the seaboard from the broad and fertile lands of the Middle West. Daniel Boone had blazed a way that later became known as the Wilderness Trail and another one had

The Cumberland Road Today crosses the nation and is well known as Route 40.

been cut through the forests of southern Pennsylvania by General Braddock in 1755, while Forbes had made another into the Pittsburgh area. None of them, however, were anything more than trails of the crudest kind. They served for trains of packhorses, although Braddock is supposed to have gotten some wagons through on his ill-fated expedition.

But with the excitement caused by the toll road movement all over the East the Federal Government itself caught the fever, made a careful survey and started to work in the early 1800's to build a real road into the Midwest. Cumberland, Maryland, was selected as the eastern terminus: this was on the Potomac River and would thus take advantage of water transportation up the river from the coast to the head of navigation and thence by the new road to what is now Wheeling, West Virginia, on the Ohio River, and into the very heart of the nation.

In 1818 the road was opened for traffic, and compared to all other roads in the country at that time it was far superior. It was sixty feet wide and wound through the mountains in a way that would do credit to our modern road-builders. A little later it was extended west to Indianapolis. Today this road goes every inch of the way from the Atlantic Ocean at Atlantic City to the Pacific Ocean and is well known as Route 40.

3

The Sleeping Giant
Stirs: The Beginnings of
American Business

The American victory at Yorktown in 1781 and the treaty that Franklin, Jay, and Adams brought back from Paris two years later removed the political yoke of England from our shoulders, but, as we were painfully to discover, it did not make us a nation. Having got rid of our royal rulers, we found ourselves faced with the entirely new problem of governing ourselves —rather like a young soldier who is discharged from the army and finds that he no longer has his life regulated by military discipline, his uniform prescribed and provided, and all his actions mapped out for him; he has to face the world on his own and fit himself into the economic life of the community in a way that will win the respect of his fellows. Such was the dilemma of the new republic.

Its territory was imperial in dimension, stretching from the Atlantic Ocean to the Mississippi River and from the Great Lakes to the Spanish-held Floridas— about a million square miles, or nearly the equal of all western Europe including the British Isles. The population was something over three million, including more than half a million black slaves and an unknown number of indentured servants or redemptioners. Most of the population was of English ancestry, but there were also sizable groups of Dutch, German, Irish,

French, and Swedes. Of the larger cities Philadelphia had a population of about 40,000, while New York and Boston were somewhat smaller.

New England exported fish and imported from the West Indies molasses to be made into rum; it also had a large ship-building industry. The middle Atlantic colonies exported furs and lumber, and the South cotton, tobacco, and indigo. But except for ship-building there was still no manufacturing, since it had been largely forbidden in Colonial times. Nearly every home could produce some kind of manufactured item but not on a large scale. As for commerce, it was the peddler who was still the principal link between the native or foreign source of supply and the consumer, and he would remain so for several generations.

What had become the United States might easily have remained thirteen small individual nations. Most men's interests were purely local, in spite of Washington's having had a continental army; and the very idea of creating centralized power brought to the American individualist fears of a return of a king who could deprive him of his rights or privileges. Yet some central authority had to be set up. The old Articles of Confederation that had served so inadequately during the Revolution had given the Continental Congress nothing more than advisory powers; it could not levy the simplest tax. If it had had the powers to commandeer food and clothing for its army, Washington and his troops need not have suffered as they did at Valley Forge. Enough necessities had existed, but no one had had the power to allocate them.

And so a group of men met in Philadelphia in the spring of 1787 to draft the Constitution. On paper, at least, we were a nation, with a president who had more power than many a king, and a system of checks and balances that was to work remarkably well. But a stable economic system had still to be developed.

Almost overnight we realized that if we wanted to build a factory and turn out a hundred gadgets a day we could do it, subject to no law other than the age-old one of supply and demand. If we had a feeling that we would be better off if we moved away from the

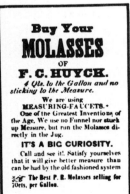

coast into the interior somewhere we were perfectly free to pack our possessions on a packhorse and head west where we could get a fresh start.

A group of mechanics and tradesmen in Baltimore in 1789, even before the last signature was on the Constitution, petitioned Congress to make them "independent in fact, as well as in name" by imposing a duty on all imported articles that they were apt to want to make themselves. The Baltimore petition was followed immediately by similar requests from each of our large cities. We were growing up fast. In fact the petitions just spoken of were made in April, 1789, and on July 4 of the same year Congress passed the first Revenue Bill "for the encouragement and protection of manufacturers" and President Washington signed it into law.

In 1790 the Patent Office was created, a fact that is packed with significance; the lawmakers knew that every town and village in the new nation was seething with mechanical ideas and improvements that would require the protective action of the government if invention was to be encouraged. Clocks were beginning to be made in Connecticut and Pennsylvania. Hand tools such as axes were being made in Massachusetts and plows in New York. Eastern Pennsylvania gunsmiths were making improvements in firearms, and even jewelry, something we had never dreamed of making here, was coming out of a factory in Newark, New Jersey.

Odell Shepard in his delightful *Connecticut, Past and Present* has a sentence that seems to me to describe, about as well as it can be done, this period in our history when our sleeping giant was waking up. "Connecticut had been a blackened fire, a steel spring pressed down, an arrow drawn to the head. Now, all at once, she was making buttons, pins and needles, plated silverware, beaver hats, combs, broadcloth and innumerable clocks."

Sporadic attempts had been made from time to time for many years to establish the textile business on a commercial basis here and there about the country, but the making of cloth of all kinds was one of England's prized industries and she had fought tooth and nail every feeble attempt we had made to get into it. As early as 1788 the first woolen mill had been set up in Hartford, while the year before the first cotton mill had been attempted in Beverly, Massachusetts, to make corduroy and bed ticking.

But in 1790 the first Arkwright machinery for spinning cotton in this country was set up in Providence by Almy and Brown. The greater part of the credit for this must go to a young fellow named Samuel Slater. Slater spent several years working in the cotton mills of England, apparently with the idea of not only learning the business, but also bringing duplicates of their machinery back here. But with England's everlasting vigilance about such things he had to return empty handed. He was unable to bring back the working drawings he had made, much less the models he had prepared, and of course no actual machinery. But young Mr. Slater had a memory that today would be described as photographic, for when he got back to Providence he was able to construct a complete duplicate of the English machinery. It worked so well that to this day Slater is called the father of the industry in this country.

His mill worked by water power, of course: it spun the fibers into thread or yarn; the weaving of either of

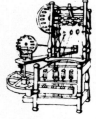

ARKWRIGHT
SPINNING MACHINE

Samuel Slater.

these into finished cloth, however, continued to be done in the home for some years. Not until 1813 was the power-driven loom to appear. In that year Francis C. Lowell of Waltham, Massachusetts, managed to construct one that worked, and for the first time in our history the spinning of yarn and its subsequent weaving into cloth, all by mechanical power, could be done under one roof.

Winning the Revolution had given us our political freedom, but it remained for the War of 1812 to give us our economic and commercial freedom from Great Britain. For two centuries she had tried by every means she could think of to make us a captive market for her manufacturers. Now that the formal Treaty of Ghent was signed and she was no longer able to control either our shipping or our manufacturing, she came up with

The overhead shafts of these power looms were all driven by one water wheel.

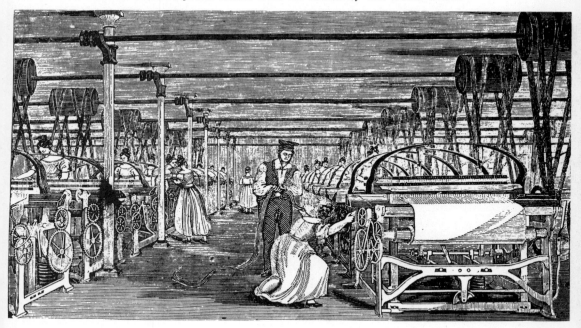

one last trick. This consisted of sending shipload after shipload of fine English-made tools, hardware, textiles of every kind, cutlery, and even needles and pins to each one of our big eastern port cities and auctioning them off for any price they would bring.

Lord Brougham's statement in Parliament at the time makes no effort whatever to conceal England's intentions. "It was worth the while to incur a loss upon the first exportations in order to stifle the rising manufacturers in the United States, which the war had forced into existence, contrary to the usual order of things."

At this point we might easily picture scenes of torchlight parades of patriotic citizens and midnight meetings of patriots designed to protect our infant industries by ignoring the sudden presence of well-known English

Lowell, Massachusetts, at Pawtucket Falls of the Merrimack River, was the first American mill city. *New York Public Library.*

goods suddenly available at a small fraction of their normal price. We might even imagine repetitions of the Boston Tea Party with crates of cutlery, pewter, and woolen goods being consigned to the bottom of our harbors by bands of "Indians"; but the fact is that nothing even faintly resembling either of these events happened.

The shipping interests of New England, and to some extent those of the middle Atlantic states, had nearly starved to death during the entire period of the war. English ships had kept our ports so bottled up that the businessmen of New England had never displayed any great interest in what they called "Mr. Madison's War." Consequently when they suddenly found the piers piled high with English goods that could be bought for half the normal price and sold overnight at a big profit—*they bought them*. The importers, the merchants, and the peddlers went on a spree of buying. Crates of the best English pewter were sold on the pier as soon as they were landed. Case after case of genuine Sheffield silver was snapped up by the importers and before nightfall was being readily sold into the surrounding homes by peddlers. Tons of the finest tools from Birmingham were on their way into our Middle West as fast as wagons could carry them. Locks and keys, nails and screws, razors and scissors poured into our ports and were sold for whatever they would bring —the result of England's effort to "stifle the rising manufacturers in the United States."

As we look back on this hectic period in our history (it lasted only about one year), we wonder how the canny English could have been so shortsighted. They could not hope to continue selling to us at a loss: that cannot be done indefinitely by anyone. Beyond any doubt the year 1816 was not to be a record one for our many small manufacturers and it is perfectly possible that some of them did get discouraged. But the records show that for each one that did three and even four new ones appeared, a pace that was to continue at an even faster rate in the generations ahead.

In 1793 the South produced 487,000 pounds of cotton. Just three years later the South produced 6,250,000 pounds. This means that in two short years our southern states multiplied their production of cotton by *thirteen*, a figure so phenomenal it would be hard to believe without knowing why and how. And if you are not impressed with this increase of thirteen times, I suggest you apply the same multiple to, let us say, automobiles. We have difficulty in dodging them on the streets *now*, so can you imagine what the streets would be like if we had thirteen times as many to dodge?

Here is the way it happened. As a money-making crop cotton had been slowly growing all during the early colonial period, but it was far behind tobacco. England took virtually all of our crop and would have taken much more had we produced it. But the difficulty was this: one man could easily raise enough cotton in a normal growing season to make about five bales (2,000 to 2,500 pounds), but before he could bale it he had to *take the seeds out of it*. Each little cotton boll had in it a dozen or more seeds, each about the size of a small pea, and they clung to the cotton fibers so tightly that each seed had forcibly to be pulled out by hand, which meant an incredible amount of labor. In fact the labor was such that one man would actually have to spend *twelve hours a day every day for a full twelve months* doing it.

Of course in practice most of the cotton was raised on large plantations where dozens of slaves did the work. This cut the time away down but did not reduce the amount of labor at all. It simply meant that the large plantations could ship this year's crop this year.

But a young fellow up in New Haven, Connecticut, was to change all this. Eli Whitney was born in Westborough, Massachusetts. He had taken the usual classical courses at Yale and graduated in the class of 1792. In the following year he headed south, probably with some idea of teaching school: at any rate one evening when he was a dinner guest in the home of General Nathanael Greene, near Savannah, the perennial problem of getting the seeds out of the cotton came up for discussion. It was a perfectly safe after-dinner topic among the men, as everybody could voice an opinion on it with no possibility of offending anyone, but, so far as we know now, nobody had ever done anything about it.

However Mr. Whitney is said to have asked a servant to bring him a boll of cotton with the seeds in it and he spent the rest of the evening meditatively pulling the seeds out of it.

No one now seems to know at just what moment Mr. Whitney suddenly stopped thinking about how to get the seed *out of the cotton* and began to think of how to get the *cotton away from the seeds*. But we do know that within one week of this fateful evening he had put together a little contrivance about the size of a hat box that was so effective that its principles took hold immediately. But insofar as Mr. Whitney's fortunes went, the very simplicity of the thing was his downfall. He took a patent on it, to be sure, but no conceivable patent could give him any real protection, as any semi-skilled mechanic could make another just like it once he had seen one. Faster than a prairie fire the cotton gin spread across the South. Hundreds of them went into operation, turning out cotton ready to put in bales in minutes instead of hours. Almost overnight cotton acreage doubled and trebled and kept on increasing for many years. The price of cotton went down, of

Whitney's original cotton gin.

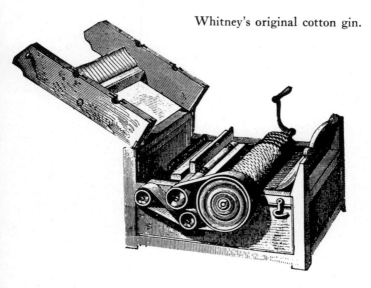

course, away down to half what it had been, but the profits went up. England could use all we could produce, and by this time our own people in New England had begun to build spinning and weaving plants to give the English a race; a race that we eventually won. While Eli Whitney was never able to make a direct profit out of his patent he did not lose out entirely, as some years later both North and South Carolina awarded him a sum of money that, while not large, was decidedly more than just a moral profit.

**WHITNEY
MILLING MACHINE**

Now the United States had manufactured goods and a basic crop that brought huge profits to the South. With an increasing abundance of merchandise to sell and money to buy with, the peddler became an even more important figure—and he had the consumer and the manufacturer on his side. Some roads had already been built; now the manufacturer, realizing that he depended on the peddler and the peddler depended on transport, added his voice to the clamor for more roads. In the East he could easily saturate the immediate area with his product, and if he did not push on and on into more and more distant markets his business was going to be limited.

Consequently from about 1790 to around 1840 America went on a road-building binge. That is just what it was—everybody became road-conscious. A new turnpike would be proposed and overnight the capital to build it would be oversubscribed. In 1792 when a turnpike from Philadelphia out to Lancaster (68 miles) was proposed, 2,267 shares of stock in it were sold within twelve hours.

Connecticut built or improved a dozen turnpikes. Incidentally the Connecticut Yankees are given credit for the custom that was to become rather widespread for some years—that of allowing a farmer a credit on his taxes in return for his maintaining the road near his home.

The combined effect of all this road-building had an effect on our economy that was far greater than any-

Pawtucket, and all of New England, was never the same after Slater set up the first successful factory system.

body had dreamt about. It created the carriage-making industry.

Back in 1768 a couple of Irishmen from Dublin came over to New York. Instead of joining the police force (or whatever its equivalent was at that time), they set up a factory to make carriages. They seem to have brought with them a few skilled carriage-makers. They built a shop down about where one of the piers of Brooklyn Bridge now is. Fortunately we have one of their announcements to the public which is very interesting.

"We are prepared to make coaches, chariots, landaus, phaetons, post chaises, curricle chairs, sedans, and sleighs—5% below importation prices."

We have no record of how well they succeeded on this venture, but we may guess that they did fairly well. In the middle of the eighteenth century carriages were just beginning to filter down from the exclusive use of royalty to the nobility and even a few of the wealthy merchant classes. And in the New York of that period enough wealth existed for at least a few individuals to acquire the distinction of appearing in carriages. The streets were too full of potholes and tree stumps to allow for much speed but if you kept the horses to a walk you could get around all right. We can not be sure that this carriage plant was the very first of its kind in this country but the chances are that it was. An old record in Boston dated 1753 indicates that in that year Boston had seven pleasure carriages per thousand of population, and so we may estimate that at least seventy families were enjoying the prestige of going around town in a horse-drawn carriage of some kind. I have been unable to find any record of carriages being made in Boston at this period, so they must have been imported.

The curricle chair referred to in the New York advertisement was quite new at that time: it was nothing more than the somewhat older sedan chair mounted on two wheels and pulled by one or two horses. The old

sedan chair was just an elaborate chair with a roof over
it and a door on one side for the lone passenger to sit
and look languidly out at the common people. It was
supported by long poles carried on the shoulder of
two servents; and if you feel that this was an undue
amount of man power to devote to carrying just one
man, don't forget our automobiles; we commonly use
the power of three hundred horses to carry one man.

The public in the 1790's, particularly the businessmen with money to invest, were buying into either a
new toll road or a new carriage factory faster than
either could be built. New Haven had five carriage
plants while Hartford had more than that; Albany,
Boston—in fact every community of any size at all—
seem suddenly to have decided that they could no
longer be thoroughly happy if they did not have a
carriage plant every few blocks.

Under the name carriage is included any kind of
vehicle designed to be drawn by some kind of draft
animal. This would include, of course, the two-wheeled
cart that was to be the standard equipment for both
the farmer and the mechanic for more than a century.
The cart with only two wheels had a definite advantage
over a vehicle that traveled on four wheels. If the
wheels were fairly large they could get over a road
that would stop anything on four wheels. This fact became so well known that for a couple of generations
during the nineteenth century certain roads were desig-
nated as "cart roads" and you would be smart if you
counted your wheels before venturing on one of them.
But by no means all of the two-wheeled vehicles were
carts. The curricle chair with its two wheels never
won much acceptance over here: it seemed to smack a
little too much of royalty for our democratic tastes.
But in a big way we went for the post chaise, in spite
of the fact that it came very directly from the French
nobility. This was a neat little carriage designed for
either one or two passengers. It had a calash top that
could be folded back whenever the proud owner wanted
to make sure he would be recognized. Of course the
early models had no springs whatever and consequently
must have been a bit bouncy, but who cared? You were

riding in a carriage, and as a status symbol that was worth all the bumps the worst road could produce.

However, by common consent, we quickly took all the French out of post chaise, changing it to shay and later to one-horse shay, and it remained just that for a great many years after it had ceased to indicate social position.

This whole binge of carriage building and road making must have been exciting to the people of that day. For all practical purposes traveling on wheels was as new and strange to the people of that time as traveling by air was to be in the early twentieth century. To be sure, the old Romans had had their chariots drawn by two and even three horses, but the Romans had had their baths too—both these things had disappeared in the intervening centuries.

But along with the rapid development of vehicles

The one horse shay, an early symbol of social position.

for pleasure went possibly even more ingenuity and inventiveness in the creation of vehicles for business. Wagons in a variety limited only by the imagination of the maker were pouring out of the factories. Today the automobile manufacturers pride themselves on coming out with new models once a year, but in the feverish period we are looking at the production of new models had no relation to the calendar at all: they appeared as fast as the makers could put them together and find buyers.

In the business of peddling, this period was the fork in the road, the moment when the peddler had to make the decision to continue selling the small items that he could carry in a tin trunk strapped to his back or invest in a horse and wagon. If he decided on a wagon he immediately had a number of other important decisions to make. He could buy a small open-to-the-sky model that would carry several hundred pounds of a big variety of items, if they were not too large, and still leave room for his old trunk in the rear; he was sure to find many a spot where he could not go with the wagon or, the farmer too busy to come out to it, he would shoulder the old trunk and go after him. A piece of canvas to tie over the whole top of the wagon would keep the rain off his goods. This outfit would require about the smallest investment of any of the wagons and had the advantage of a high resale price if he found he could not make it pay off. He could carry some of the smaller farm tools if he could find a mechanic who would make some for him. Picks and shovels and all such tools were badly needed by the settlers inland, but mechanics able to make them in worthwhile quantities were hard to find. Even the road-building contractor of the period with a crew of a hundred men had to carry a portable blacksmith shop along to make the tools for his men right on the job.

The more daring peddler could decide to go in for a single specialty line like textiles if he cared to. This would require a radically different type of wagon. It would have rolls of cloth packed closely on the floor of the wagon to be displayed later on racks on each side. The display rack was simply a number of rolls

of cloth mounted on rods, one above the other, like wrapping paper in an old-fashioned store. This wagon would have flaps on the sides that would fold up on the roof when the peddler was open for business and fold down to close in the sides when the weather was bad. In the period around 1800 virtually all of the cloth used in the homes was made in the home: the spinning wheel, the dye pot, and the loom were standard equipment everywhere, and it was to be a long-drawn-out battle between "store cloth" and homespun. "Homespun" meant that the yarn or thread was homespun, but yarn was only a raw material. It had to be woven into cloth before you could wear it; the cloth might more accurately be called "homewoven." But homespun it is and nothing now can ever change it. The term "linsey-woolsey" came into the language at about the same time, and it made complete sense because it meant a type of homespun that was made from a mixture of linen and wool.

The fine new wagons with rolls and rolls of gaily colored ginghams and calicos were calculated to dazzle the eyes of the pioneer housewife. She could go out to the wagon and, standing on a stool the peddler carried for the purpose, she could unroll a yard or so of material, drape it over her shoulder and imagine what it would mean to have a whole new dress made of it. Then she could repeat this process with each roll on his rack, comparing each one with her own product that took so many, many hours to make—and even then it would be only homespun. Did she dare use up all her egg money on this bit of finery? If her answer was yes, it was a simple matter for the peddler to cut off the required yardage. Of course he would always come up with a special price on a remnant, and there were no rules that defined how much yardage constituted a remnant: it might be twenty or even thirty yards, enough for her to make clothes for the whole family.

Sure enough, a few weeks later the small daughters would appear in new dresses and before long the boys would be showing off new shirts, and even Maw and Paw—all from the very same roll of material. If nature had not given the members of the family a pronounced resemblance, a little old-fashioned economy made up for it.

Of course the peddler of cloth was by no means the only type that developed specialized wagons. During the entire nineteenth century new kinds appeared in unending variety. Probably the most spectacular was the huge freight carrier, later to be called the Conestoga wagon.

It has often been said that the Conestoga wagon and the Concord coach were the two most perfect vehicles

The Conestoga wagon, designed to carry up to six tons, was a huge vehicle even by today's standards.

ever produced here. Each was perfection itself for the time and circumstances. The Conestoga was the product of Germans from the Palatinate who settled much of eastern Pennsylvania from early in the eighteenth century right on through the period of the Revolution. Large numbers of them came to Lancaster County, particularly the town of Conestoga. Most of them were farmers, but a few of them were mechanics of rare ability who left a lasting mark on our society.

However the wagon that was destined to spread the name of the town all over the country must have been the product of many individuals because, unlike the Kentucky rifle that sprang from the same group of people at the same time, the name of no particular craftsmen is linked with the Conestoga.

It was a huge vehicle even by today's standards, designed to carry up to six tons of freight over mountains and across streams. It was drawn by six powerful horses guided by a driver who either walked beside them, with the reins in his hands, or rode a wheelhorse. The wagon was made of sturdy oak and the floor was tilted up in front and in the rear too. This reduced the possibility of heavy freight shifting around on steep grades. The wheels were five to six feet in diameter and the heavy steel tire would be from six inches to as many as ten inches wide.

Six or seven arched bows of hickory crossed the wagon, the smallest in the middle: these supported a sheet of canvas to protect the contents. Attached either to the rear or on one side was a box filled with food for the horses and blankets for the driver, along with a bundle of cold beef, ham, and usually some jerked venison for the road. The blankets were necessary, as frequently the driver would sleep either in the wagon or alongside of the road. On occasions when he did stop at an inn he scorned the use of a soft bed: he and a dozen other drivers preferred to roll up in their blankets on the floor with their feet toward the fire. Invariably the body of the wagon was painted in the gayest bright blue while the upper parts were finished in a brilliant red.

Driving one of these vehicles gave the driver a status

far above any other driver on the road: he was the hero of the small boys as he rumbled into a small town with the bells on his horses jingling and the highly polished brass glistening in the sunlight.

It is not to be supposed that this wagon reached its peak of perfection all at once: this was never true. The first attempts to design a big freight carrier must have been made about 1750: undoubtedly improvements were made from year to year as experience demonstrated their need. A rather informative comment on them, and particularly on the roads of the period, was the fact that the toll roads had a sliding scale of rates that varied with the load and the number of horses plus the width of the tires. If the tires were six inches wide or more some toll roads gave them free passage. Looking back at it this seems very sensible; for when we remember that the early roads were little more than worn paths through the mud with no hard surface at all, a narrow tire would cut deeply into it while a great broad tire would act like a roller, tending to smooth out the surface.

The Conestoga wagon and its picturesque drivers have long since disappeared from the scene, but they enriched our language with at least one word that is likely to stay with us. The word is of course "stogie", which still means a big, roughly made cigar of cheap tobacco.

4

How Peddlers Lived

The way a peddler lived depended very much on the kind of peddler he was, and there were many kinds. If he carried his pack on his back or rode his horse he would have to find his food and night's lodging as best he could—at the home of a settler or, when travel had developed as new roads spread throughout the eastern United States, at the many inns that sprang up along the highways; and the time came when, lacking a vehicle of his own, he could travel by stagecoach if his load was not too cumbersome.

By the early nineteenth century the day of the wagon peddler had arrived. A wagon peddler might carry general merchandise—small items we call notions— all in a trunk in his wagon. Elsewhere in the wagon he might have books and other printed matter, brooms and wooden dishes, tools, and even a few iron kettles —anything he could find a market for.

Some peddlers carried bulky items such as washing machines, corn-shellers, winnowing machines, spinning wheels and looms, organs, well pumps, plows, and even furniture; they might specialize in one of these and nothing else. Then there were the specialty peddlers whose wares have now become of such interest— if they have survived—that we will look at them separately; these include, for example, tinware and clocks.

There were also peddlers of wagons and carriages. They could be seen on almost any main route: a dozen or more vehicles tied together and pulled by a big, husky team, each wagon with a bell attached and a sign telling its story. Horses and mules and even oxen were sold in the same way; and a string that included all three animals could be seen now and then, although this was not very practical since the slow-moving ox would reduce the distance that a string could cover in a day.

A peddler was usually welcome at the home of virtually any settler. In the first place his goods were needed, his news from the city was eagerly awaited, and isolated pioneers were always glad to have company. He did not have the social status of a settled merchant, but he was by no means a tramp or a ne'er-do-well—indeed most peddlers were of respectable family background, and they were peddlers only when they were young; sooner or later, when they had found a suitable spot, they settled down. Nowadays the word peddler is somewhat derogatory. Bankers, business men, and bond salesmen apply it to themselves only when they feel sure that their listeners understand that they are in fact anything but peddlers.

But through the greater part of the nineteenth century things were not that way at all. A peddler was invited into a settler's home, seated, and given a glass of cider while the housewife called her husband from the fields and the family gathered around just to look at a man who had actually been in Marietta or Warren and could tell them all the news and gossip for miles around. Even with only a few weeks of training the peddler would have learned just about how long he could permit this to go on before he opened up his pack, or led them out to the wagon and got started on his real business in life. A reference to the smell of roasting meat at the right moment might easily result in an invitation to share the family's meal with them, or, if it was late in the day, some remark about how comfortably fixed they were with all that room would frequently enable him to sleep under a roof that night.

Some peddlers built up routes for themselves that never took them more than a hundred miles or so from home. They simply made the circuit once or twice a year and that was that. This gave them the advantage of always being familiar with the road and the people on it, but it had the disadvantage of tending to keep a fellow honest, a handicap that did not appeal to all of the trade.

A country peddler attempts to make a sale to a hesitant customer. *New York Public Library.*

But the vast majority of the peddlers chose to travel great distances. From a point in Connecticut, let us say Hartford, the peddler would load his great wagon with every single thing he could get in it or on top of it or even tied under it, and bidding good-by to his family he would start out. Sometimes he would have in mind a fairly definite route, or he might be guided from time to time by the news and gossip picked up as he went along. If he had the Middle West in mind he would work his way north along the Connecticut River into Massachusetts where he would turn west on the so-called Berkshire Trail and follow it into Albany. Leaving Albany he would travel over a succession of toll roads to Schenectady and on to Utica and the Mohawk Turnpike into the Genesee Valley and the Niagara country. This is, of course, the route that the Erie Canal was to follow shortly after this period, and a busy route it surely was.

Alice Morse Earle, in her delightful *Stage Coach and Tavern Days,* writes, "The turnpike was filled with great trading wagons: there was a tavern at every mile on the road: fifty-two within fifty miles of Albany, but there were not taverns enough to meet the demand caused by the great travel. Eighty to one hundred horses would sometimes be stabled at a single tavern." From the area around Buffalo the peddler had a choice of routes: he could follow the road hugging the south shore of Lake Erie through Cleveland and from that point on into Indiana and Illinois; or he could take passage on some kind of boat from Buffalo that would land him at Cleveland or Detroit or even farther west.

But if, instead of the Middle West, the peddler wanted to try the South, then he would follow the Connecticut River south to where it empties into Long Island Sound at Saybrook and then go west on the Boston Post Road into New York. From New York he would have to follow what we know as Route 1 today. It passed through Philadelphia, Baltimore, Richmond, and the Carolinas. In the very early days of the wagon peddler, the usual course was for him to start out on a season's trip as early in the spring as the roads would permit in the hope that by late summer he would have sold out his entire stock of goods, and also turned the goods he had taken in trade into cash, and then sold the horse and wagon. If he did this, he would probably work his way up to the nearest seaport where he would hope to make some arrangement with the captain of a coaster to take him north and home. However cases were common where a peddler *never* sold out his stock; that is to say he was constantly replacing his stock with new items that he picked up at the many small factories that were springing up everywhere. He would eventually get back to his hometown for a rest and a fresh start.

In the first quarter of the nineteenth century new factories with new items never before made here were opening up constantly, and these brought about increasing competition in all the trades. The factory making an item that was what we today would call a hit could pick and chose just what peddlers it would sell to; while the factories with somewhat less salable items might have a little trouble finding peddlers enough to take their output. Yankee ingenuity got around such things in a variety of ways, one of which was at least partially to subsidize a peddler. Here is an actual case history of one such peddler. Mr. Arthur R. Alderman, of Burlington, Connecticut, wrote me as follows in 1962:

. . . My family has resided in the town of Burlington since about 1809 and two winters ago I found some letters in an old chest dated 1816–1823 and others 1832–1845. I have carefully typed all these old letters just as written and among other things they refer to Yankee Peddlers in a few ways that may be of interest to you.

The 1816–1823 letters were written by my Great Grandfather's younger brother, Manna Alderman. He was a peddler and he names other peddlers from this town. I had always thought of the Yankee Peddlers as coming from the larger manufacturing towns until I read these letters. Manna traveled southerly to Fayetteville, North Carolina, peddling tinware and here is his contract which I found in the old chest which was his own and made by him with his initials on it.

Burlington Sept 16th 1816

Know all men by these presents that I, Elisha Dunham of Berlin, in Hartford County, State of Connecticut, do agree by these presents to pay Manna Alderman Twenty Five Dollars & one half the profits that shall arise on tin and other goods at the market price, per month. Said Alderman on his part is to peddle in North Carolina & its vissinity all kinds of artacles that is lawful to be sold & the said Alderman am to find own Horse & Wagon & Soforth.

Elisha Dunham

Manna's older brother, Truman Alderman, evidently financed both his equipment and his stock in trade— here is Truman Alderman's account of it.

May the 10th 1816, paid for the horse   50
May the 7th 1816 paid for the Harness   16
May the 13th 1816 paid for the waggon   81
August the 14th 1818 paid for trading Artacles   143
                                                          ———
                                                          290

At this point the present Mr. Alderman explains as follows:

Elisha Dunham was a manufacturer of tinware and like manufacturers of other goods sent peddlers out under contract similar to the above to find a market for their goods. The Hotchkiss clock was made in Burlington at that time and peddled far and wide by the peddlers. A Hotchkiss clock is a valuable collector's item now if one can be found.

The present Mr. Alderman further explains, "In the letters [I found in the chest] were mentioned as follows":

Israel Beckwith

Lot Beckwith   "went to the southwest for Lowrey & Norton at $200 per year"

Samuel Beckwith   "Did well—making 6 to $700"

Orrin Upson   "did poorly—losing horse and being sick some"

Orren Fuller   "went way into Georgia—cleared above 300 for himself"

Michael More   "went to the southwest"

Abijah Catlin   of "Harrington" (Harwinton)

The present Mr. Alderman further explains:

Elisha Dunham apparently went bankrupt shortly after Manna went on the road and Manna was left stranded in Fayetteville North Carolina. However according to the letters he settled there, cleared land, built a home, taught school, made corn cob pipes, chests, wagons, harness etc. He married and came home to visit in the autumn of 1823 and died almost immediately upon his arrival of Typhoid fever leaving a widow and child in Fayetteville.

Here is Manna's first letter home:

Mr. Gilman [Mr. Gilman may have been a friend Manna made on

71

the road somewhere who went along for the ride] & I set out the 21
day of September—both of us did not have 6 dollars in cash before
we got to N.Y. we was near out of money and we went & trading
one day I got about 2 dollars and he got 1 dollar. We finally got over
the river at N.York—it is useless for me to write the particulars all
the way. I lamed my horse so that I lay still several days—this was
done about 500 miles from home. 9 weeks from the 21 of Sept I
arrived at North Carolina and in 3 weeks more I arrived at Fayett-
ville. When I arrived I heard that Mr Dunham had his property
tached & taken from him

Mr. Alderman gives one more interesting note: "It
is interesting to note that by the 1832–1845 letters a
sister of Manna migrated with her husband and family
in 1832 to Ohio which was known then as New Connecticut. Her son, Edward Woodruff, carried out the
Yankee peddler trade from Ohio by getting his trading articles from Burlington (Hotchkiss Clocks) and
peddling in the Indiana and Illinois areas." Mr. Alderman further writes: "In another series of letters from
my wife's family I read of Burlington Yankee peddlers
named Ariel Foot, L. Atwater and Seth Wiard peddling in Pittsburgh and Philadelphia. This letter is
dated May 1st 1832. They write that they have a 'grat
meny goods on hand that must be sold and not returned
for goods are a falin very fast and fore that reason i
must peddel into the sity if i have my helth & good
luck.'"

Except for his untimely death Manna's case was
probably not at all uncommon: cases of peddlers finding themselves stranded far from home due to some
failure at the base must have been numerous.

The names of the peddlers mentioned are every one
of them as Yankee as any set of names could be. Each
of the family names listed is still common in New England but the biblical first names have largely passed out
of use.

No less than eight young men from the (at that
time) little village of Burlington were peddlers, and
we have no reason to suppose that the eight he mentioned were the only young men there that had taken
to peddling.

We know that Meriden, Connecticut (a bit larger
than Burlington at the time), had no less than forty

peddlers a year based there, and in 1829 Hartford had as many as sixty.

The fur-trader was not the same kind of salesman as the peddler. He did not collect merchandise in the East and sell it in the back-country settlements; rather, he went out on unmapped trails to find his merchandise. Nevertheless, like the peddler, he was a commercial agent, the first to penetrate the vast areas of the Middle West; he opened the way for the peddlers who soon outnumbered him greatly, and he traded with them; and so he was vitally linked in the nation's early commerce.

It may sound strange to say that the growth of the fur business was drastically affected by a change in the prevailing styles of hats worn by men, but it seems to be the fact.

The fur of the beaver had been used during much of the eighteenth century in making men's hats. The fur itself was sheared from the hide and made into felt, and out of this the popular tricorn was shaped. But the French Revolution, beginning in 1789, caused a revolution in masculine styles in dress that was to make vast differences in the appearance of men all over the civilized world. The change did not happen overnight: in fact it took a dozen years; but by the very early 1800's the shapely masculine legs encased in silk stockings below satin breeches buckled at the knee slowly disappeared from the streets of Paris, London, and our own big cities. The satin breeches gave way

THE FUR TRADERS

The first large center of hat manufacturing was in Danbury, Connecticut.

to long trousers, made of more prosaic materials, reaching to the ankle, or just above it, where they were held down by a strap passing under the boot (see any picture of Uncle Sam). Just why the tailors of the period did not allow the new-fangled trouser leg to go clear down to the instep as they do now is not definitely known, but I would hazard a guess it was because of the muddy roads. At any rate, the new style seems to have been accepted by the common people in both Europe and over here ten to twenty years before wealthy citizens were willing to adopt it. For some reason that is wide open to speculation, the common people here were wearing the new styles years before our presidents saw fit to lay aside the old classic knee breeches; in fact James Madison, who served from 1809 to 1817, was the first of our presidents to wear long trousers, and he wore them infrequently and reluctantly.

But with the new style in trousers went a radically new kind of hat. At first it was a little truncated cone with a narrow brim. But each year it grew taller until by the early 1800's the ribbon was moved up to the top and an extension put on top of that like an inverted cone, with the ribbon acting like a belt constricting it in the middle. This produced the plug hat, which was to grow larger and larger for many years. It is the one most of us associate with the Charles Dickens type of Christmas pictures.

All this had a very important effect on the fur business in this country because obviously one of these huge hats required five or six times as much beaver fur as the old prerevolutionary chapeaux did. So the call went out from the hat-manufacturers in Europe for beaver and more beaver, and the number of men engaged in trapping the animal doubled and doubled again. The beaver is an animal that must be trapped. If he is shot he sinks to the bottom of the pond he lives in and that is the end of him and his pelt.

So from the early 1800's on, until after the Civil War, the skin of the beaver with all its lovely soft fur on it was the number one objective of hundreds of trappers. They usually operated in teams of two and

sometimes in larger groups, although the lone trapper
was quite common too. Beaver was his main object
because he was sure of selling all he could get and the
price would probably be higher than it was the year
before. However he did not pass up an opportunity
to bring down a deer: he could eat the deer and get
at least a small return for its hide. He skinned the animals as fast as he took them and in the spring loaded
them on his back, or on a packhorse, and started for the

A drawing by Frederic Remington depicts a fur train. *New York Public Library.*

nearest settlement where each hide had a price on it
and where he could exchange his pack for all the things
he needed and have enough money left over for some
frontier whiskey. At the settlement canoes or rafts were
loaded with the accumulated catch and taken to an
established trading post, such as the American Fur
Company's at Mackinac, or to Fort Niagara.

What the various skins were worth in goods of the
period and locality are shown in the schedule below.

1 man's shirt—plain ...... 1 Beaver Pelt or 1 Buck and 1 Doeskin.

1 man's shirt with ruffles......... 2 Beaver skins or 3 Buckskins

1 large blanket .... 2 Beaver skins or 3 Buckskins

1 Pr Women's socks............ 1 Buckskin

1 pound Gunpowder .... 1 Buckskin

1 "fathem" Calico .... 1 Beaver pelt or 1 Buck and
1 doeskin.

1 lg. silk handkerchief........... 1 Buck or 1 Doeskin

1 Red " " .... 2 Beaver pelts or 3 Buckskins

2 "fathem" of Ribbon........... 1 Buck

Brass kettles were sold by weight—one pound of kettle for one pound of Beaver pelts.

1 gal. Tin kettle............... 2 Bucks

Silver wrist bands............... 2 Bucks

Silver Arm Bands............... 4 Beaver or 5 bucks

This is the exchange list at a post in the Niagara area shortly before the Revolution and should not be taken as an average for the whole Middle West. It was before the price of beaver pelts really began to climb. Incidentally, I do not think we have to look any farther to find the origin of our slang expression for one dollar.

Since the beaver pelt was to mount in exchange value year after year for more than two generations, the pioneer settlers would trap every beaver they could find and have them on hand to offer the peddler when he pulled up his wagon at the door of the cabin. You can be sure the peddler knew the current value of a beaver pelt far better than the isolated settler did, and it is not hard to imagine him telling the pioneer that the trading posts were so loaded up with beaver he would not be surprised if they would not take any more of them in, at least until they had been able to find a buyer for the huge heap of them they had.

The peddler and the trapper were the only large groups of people who were almost constantly on the move in early America. The trapper, as we have seen, played a more or less lone hand: he and his partner would spend an entire winter holed up in some isolated cabin, perhaps for six months at a time, completely out of touch with civilization and when he did go in to the nearest settlement it was to stay only a short time and then return to the cabin.

The peddler, on the other hand, came from a settled area where manufactured goods would be available and where he would mingle with other people. When he started out on a trip that might easily take him away from home for more than six months, he was intensely interested in the people he called on, because only to the extent that he knew people and their problems could he supply their wants. He was sociable out of necessity and became a trained observer for the same reason. But there was more to his work than merely selling goods: by the very nature of his long, extended trips into areas only then being settled, he was in position to disseminate vast amounts of useful information to would-be pioneers in the East who needed some of the firsthand information only he could give. He would know the areas where the soil was good and the people were prosperous: and who could better point out the best route for reaching that area than the man who had just covered it?

The peddler from New England was indeed the advance scout for the thousands of his fellow New Englanders who settled the entire western end of New York State and flowed over into western Pennsylvania and Ohio around the turn of the century.

We have seen how the rivers flowing into the Atlantic became channels for the peddlers working out of the port cities in the early 1700's. They paddled canoeloads of goods up the rivers to the settlements and soon used rafts with sails. The same thing happened, in reverse, on the Ohio River and its larger tributaries in the early 1800's. Before 1819, when the new National Road opened from Cumberland across the mountains to Wheeling on the Ohio, and thereby made transportation by wagon practicable, goods had been carried almost entirely by packhorses. At least two organizations of some size were in the business of carrying goods by that means: one of them is said to have had close to five hundred packhorses on the road every day. When the wonderful National Road opened, however, with its sixty-foot-wide expanse of hard and relatively smooth surface, this number multiplied several times and the rates for carrying one hundred pounds across the mountains was cut in half.

However, when a pack train arrived at Wheeling, and the precious packs were unloaded, the broad stretches of the Ohio River lay ahead—more than five hundred miles of almost effortless floating downstream, and still more than that if the peddlers wished to continue down the Mississippi. Late in the eighteenth century peddlers in both Wheeling and Pittsburgh were packing goods into canoes and onto rafts and then onto keelboats and still later onto small steamboats and going downriver. A loud horn would announce the arrival

A supply train over the mountain. *New York Public Library.*

A boat carrying furs is paddled up the Missouri. *New York Public Library.*

of a "store boat" and the housewife would hurry down
to the pier to replace the cups that had all been broken
or buy some other commodity. She might desperately
need some gingham for the new dress she had been
promised, and she could spend a half hour or more in-
dulging that age-old feminine joy that today we call
shopping.

Up to Civil War times these store boats became
more and more elaborate: they had neat counters and
shelves along which the housewife could do her shopping in a leisurely manner without quite the same guilty
feeling she used to have when the peddler stopped his
wagon at her door and she held his exclusive attention
for some time without buying anything.

Reminders of the days when the Ohio was the great-
est artery of trade in the Middle West can still be seen

in Cincinnati and probably in Marietta too. They consist of small houses built entirely of lumber sawed into boards far upriver in Pittsburgh or Wheeling, made into rafts right on the spot, loaded with a family and all their household goods, and floated downstream day after day until a settlement was reached that looked like a good location for a new home. Tying up at the bank of the river, the family picked a site for their home and then *built it out of the raft* that they would no longer need.

Fur skins are examined at a trading depot. *New York Public Library.*

5

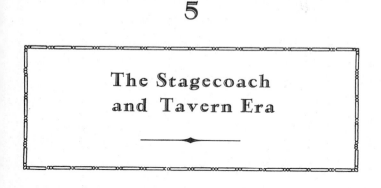

The Stagecoach
and Tavern Era

It was the demands of the peddlers that helped to create a highway system in the East; and once a network of roads came into existence public transport began with the era of stagecoaches and taverns. Not all travelers or guests at inns were peddlers; but by the early 1800's there were thousands of peddlers, and not all of them could sleep under their own wagons or cadge a night's lodging from a lonely settler, so a good part of an innkeeper's business depended on peddlers of various kinds.

Roads, stagecoaches, and taverns did not spring into being overnight, or even in a short time. It took a long while to get any kind of road built; then it took years of experimentation, as we have seen in the case of the Conestoga wagon, to evolve a vehicle adapted to the roads; and only then could chains of taverns begin to thrive along well-traveled routes. Until then the "Swamp Yankees"—a term applied to Connecticut Yankees by the natives of the hillier states of Massachusetts, Vermont, and New Hampshire—had to protect their goods by night from thieves, and in the back country they had to guard themselves from Indian attacks.

The exact date and place of the establishment of the first common carrier seems to have been lost over the years, and it took centuries to develop the stagecoach from the crude carriages used in England and later in the eastern cities of America. As early as 1556 the Earl of Rutland designed and built himself a boxlike coach; the box was set directly on the axles, and the going must have been rough. But it must have caused some stir in London because Queen Elizabeth ordered one for herself shortly thereafter with, we may suppose, some improvements. She went about in it for eight years, apparently without getting too discouraged, since she ordered a new model in 1564. The English nobility followed her example, and in a short time the cobblestones of the city rumbled with the clatter of a hundred coaches. A writer of the period has left us a record of early coach traffic: "Coaches jammed the streets and aided purse-cutting; that butchers could not pass with their cattle; that market-folk were hindered in bringing victuals to town; that carts and carriers were stopped; that milkmaids were flung in the dirt; that people were crowded and shrowded up against walls and stoops."

Some of the same congestion may have existed in the narrower streets of early American cities, because the English shipped some kind of "boneshaker" to their American colonies. Every royal governor over here had to have his coach; otherwise he might not be recognized in the streets and might even be mistaken for a gentleman. However, a carriage soon proved insufficient to distinguish the governor when our own men of wealth began taking to wheels. Watson in his *Annals of Philadelphia* in 1761 left us a list of the thirty-eight individuals who owned carriages in that city. There were three coaches, two landaus, eighteen chariots, and fifteen chairs. In 1772 this had increased to eighty-four carriages. The "chariots" spoken of had no resemblance to the chariots of ancient Rome. These eighteenth-century carriages were supposed to be the last word in fancy travel about town. They had doors and windows and even some clumsy springs.

But all of these carriages were meant for town travel; none at this time was designed to stand the rigors of travel between cities. True, back in 1737 an effort had been made to send a roadwagon on regular trips between Boston and Providence, but it does not seem to have carried passengers. The records also indicate that in the same year two coaches were brought in from England and an attempt made to establish a passenger-carrying service over this same road but the records are not at all clear on its success. The old accounts indicate that the first stage trip from Boston to New York was in 1765, over what has since been called the Boston Post Road. Six years before this a stage-wagon line had been set up in New York to make trips twice a week to Philadelphia. This seems to have been designed mostly for freight but they did carry some passengers on it. And we are told they made the one-way trip in three days.

The fine new National Road from Cumberland, Maryland, west to Wheeling, with every mile of it crowded at this time with home-seekers heading west, opened up with no less than four different coach lines: the National Line, the Pioneer Line, the Good Intent Line, and for some strange reason the fourth was named June Bug. The Pioneer Line seems to have expanded its service quickly, as we find it serving at least as far west as Cleveland.

The advent of the stagecoach sent us off on another binge. First came the road-building binge; now it was stagecoach lines, soon it would be canals, and soon after that it would be railroads. It is strange, when we look back, that a nation as young as ours would have so many thousands of people not only with money to invest but the faith and courage to do something constructive with it, for in the years between 1800 and about 1830 many thousands of individuals invested enormous sums in stage lines—*and,* for a few years, *made enormous profits.*

NEWS! NEWS!

AARON OLIVER, *Poſt-Rider,*

WISHES to inform the Publick, that he has extended his Route; and that he now rides thro' the Towns of *Troy, Pittſtown, Hooſick, Mapletown,* Part of *Bennington,* and *Shaftſbury, Peterſburgh, Stephentown, Greenbuſh* and *Schodack.*

All Commands in his Line will be received with Thanks, and executed with Punctuality.

He returns his ſincere Thanks to his former Cuſtomers; and intends, by unabated Diligence, to merit a Continuance of their Favours.

O'er ruggid hills, and vallies wide,
 He never yet has fail'd to trudge it;
As ſteady as the flowing tide,
 He hands about the NORTHERN BUDGET.

June 18, 1799.

In 1827 up in Concord, New Hampshire, one carriage-maker, out of the hundreds scattered all over the country, designed and built a new coach that was so perfectly adapted to its purpose that virtually overnight it made every other coach in the country obsolete. The maker of the Concord coach, which was the name in-

THE CONCORD COACH

stantly given it, started turning them out twenty-four hours a day and soon apparently made arrangements with many other carriage-makers to use his design, because in an exceedingly short time the roads became dotted with Concord coaches. So perfect was the design that seventy-five years later in the early 1900's the same coach was being produced and used in many parts of the far West where the rail lines had not yet reached.

But in the eighteen twenties and thirties the stagecoach really dominated American travel; it made travel by land relatively easy, so that for the first time an extended trip could be taken anywhere in the East. The times of departure and arrival could be known in advance and even the approximate cost. The expense of traveling between Philadelphia and Pittsburgh, a distance of 297 miles, was twenty dollars for the fare and about seven dollars for food and lodging en route. The trip took seven days.

Certain lines were given the franchise to carry the mail; usually this meant the lowest bidders. These would have the coaches that could make the fastest time and as a consequence they charged a higher fare for passengers.

The Concord Coach, first built in 1827, was used by Wells Fargo and others well into the 1900's.

Wilmington and New-Castle Mail.

THE SUBSCRIBERS respectfully inform the Public, and the Citizens of Wilmington and New-Castle in particular, that they have established a Stage for the purpose of carrying the Mail between the aforesaid places, and also for the conveyance of passengers and baggage....It will leave New-Castle for Wilmington, every morning between 6 and 7 o'clock, and arrive at D. BRINTON's Tavern, in time for passengers to take the 8 o'clock Stage for Philadelphia.

THE Stage will occasionally return to New-Castle in the forenoon, when a sufficient number of passengers offer, and back to Wilmington, and leave there every day for New-Castle after the arrival of the Philadelphia Stages.

Passengers may rest assured, that this establishment will be much safer and more expeditious than any heretofore established between those two Towns; having the best horses, and a careful driver.

JOSEPH BRINGHURST, P. M. Wilmington.
DAVID MORRISON, P. M. New-Castle.

Wilmington, Delaware.

The editor of the *Providence Gazette* wrote, "We were rattled from Providence to Boston in four hours and fifty minutes—if anyone wants to go faster he may send to Kentucky and charter a streak of lightning."

But speed brought so much business that the fare was raised, which, in turn, brought competing lines onto the run with a lower fare and, at least on this run (Boston–Providence), the competition became so intense that one line began carrying passengers for nothing. Not to be outdone another line offered the same thing but with a free dinner at the end of the run; and their competitor capped this by offering a bottle of wine with their free dinner. Needless to say, this sort of thing had to end, and soon did in a compromise. In 1818 all the lines in the whole of eastern Massachusetts, New Hampshire, Maine, and Rhode Island combined into a syndicate called the "Eastern Stage Company," and for a few years it made fabulous profits for the stockholders. In 1832 no fewer than one hundred and six coach lines terminated in Boston. No comparable figures for New York or Philadelphia are available, but there is every reason to think that conditions in those cities were similar to New England. Boston even started a newspaper with a special appeal to the passengers of the stages; it was called *The Boston Traveler* and is still being published.

But lest you begin to think that we were becoming speed-crazy, here is a sobering note. George Washington died on December 14, 1799. An event of such importance would of course be flashed all over the country by the very fastest means possible. Just how fast this was is a bit startling—the news did not reach Boston till ten full days had elapsed (December 24). It had to be carried either by stagecoach or post-rider. It probably was by a whole series of post-riders, forerunners of the Pony Express but without any of the careful preparation that went into the Pony Express in the 1860's.

The convenience of travel by stage did great things to the amount of travel by the public, as was to be expected, and this in turn increased the demand for food and lodging along the way. In the summer a stage might make from fifteen to twenty or more miles in a day while in winter it might not be able to make more than five to ten miles from sunrise to sunset. A change of horses was planned every ten to twelve miles; the stage might stop for a full hour, while the passengers warmed themselves before the fire of an inn and their stomachs by some of the fire the landlord kept in the taproom.

ROADS AND TAVERNS

Nowadays a tavern means a saloon, a word that has fallen into disrepute. In early Colonial times it was called an "ordinary," but this word was gradually dropped and inn or tavern substituted. In the 1600's taverns were restricted to the cities, not so much by law as by the fact that very few people were to be found elsewhere. In 1714, in Boston, which had a population of ten thousand, there were thirty-four inns in operation, and probably the figures in New York and Philadelphia were comparable.

But with the establishment of turnpikes and the coming of the stagecoach the whole atmosphere of our countryside changed. No longer was a road a narrow trail through the woods, with an occasional horseman leading a packhorse or two and maybe a lone post-rider and a couple of peddlers all of the activity to be expected. On important roads connecting sizable places stages went by at intervals of minutes. If the terminus was a port city as many as fifty stages in a single day might stop on the docks to discharge passengers. Advertisements were appearing in the papers reading, "Unbelievable though it seem The Flyer will actually carry you from Boston to New York in 1 week (7 days)," "Cleveland to Pittsburgh in 30 hours," "The Flying Machine—New York to Philadelphia."

Of course this enormous increase in travel resulted in a vast increase in the number of inns and taverns along every road of importance. For many years night-driving was not attempted; the day's run would end early in the evening at a prearranged inn where the passengers would eat dinner and perhaps sample the brew of the innkeeper who usually presided in the taproom. The passengers would be told the time of departure in the morning (this was usually at least as early as five o'clock) and off they would go.

Before and during the Revolution the inns were the meeting places for the colonials, and they continued to be the scene of political gatherings from the local level on up to the national. The Raleigh Tavern in Williams-

The Raleigh Tavern in Williamsburg, Virginia has been faithfully restored. *New York Public Library*.

burg, Virginia, is one of the best known, and also one of the finest. The original tavern was burned to the ground just before the Civil War broke out, but it has been faithfully rebuilt to the smallest detail on the original foundation. The dedicated group of architects and historians did a beautiful job in the restoration, greatly aided by two fine engravings made in 1848 and a complete inventory of furnishings made in 1771. It is said that the gentlemen and ladies of the pre-Revolutionary period could return to the tavern today and have the feeling that they had not been absent more than a week or so. George Washington seems to have preferred to sleep in one of the other Williamsburg inns but his diary tells us again and again that he "dined at the Raleigh."

Public receptions were common events in this gracious old tavern. In 1775 the Williamsburg Volunteers met here to honor the return of Peyton Randolph from Philadelphia, where he had served as first President of the Continental Congress. Only one year later, when Patrick Henry was about to leave to take active command of his troops under Washington, a send-off dinner was given him here and when the Revolution ended with the Treaty of Paris this old place resounded to its rooftree with the celebration. In 1824, when Lafayette made his memorable swing around the young nation, the Raleigh was of course the scene of his Williamsburg reception. But it should not be imagined that the Raleigh was used only on formal occasions for the records show that it was the very center of much of the business of Virginia in the early days. Auctions of land and goods and slaves in front of the inn were almost daily events for a long period. Its long line of landlords acted unofficially as postal- and news-gatherers for the community; letters for overseas were deposited with the landlord, who in turn gave them to the next coachdriver headed for a seaport. And that ancient and highly honored fraternity, Phi Beta Kappa, founded in Williamsburg in 1776, held many meetings in the beautiful old Apollo Room of the Raleigh.

The number of inns in the neighborhoods of Philadelphia, Boston, and New York that were the centers

When Taverns where built to be Taverns, and _looked_ like Taverns . . .

The King of Prussia 1709 Pennsylvania

Burnham Tavern Machias, Maine 1770

The Rising Sun Fredericksburg, Va 1760

Munford Inn, Munfordsville, Ky built of 30 ft. walnut logs, 1800

Salem Tavern, Winston-Salem, N.C. 1772

The Jolly Post-Boy, Frankford, Pa. 1749

Munroe Tavern 1695 Lexington, Mass.

Fraunce's Tavern N.Y.C.

Eric Sloan's OUR VANISHING LANDSCAPE, *published by Wilfred Funk, Inc.*

of patriot activity before the Revolution are far too
numerous to mention in detail. Many served as court-
rooms for both civil and military trials, while others
were used for prisons and hospitals and, of course,
frequently for officers' headquarters.

At the old Wright Tavern in Concord British Major
Pitcairn slept the night before the battle of Concord,
and the story is told that the Major stirred his glass of
brandy that morning with a bloody finger saying that
he intended to stir the blood of the rebels that same
day. The Monroe Tavern at nearby Lexington was the
headquarters of Lord Percy on that famous April 19,
while over at the Buckman Tavern in the same town
the Minute Men were meeting. The Wayside Inn over
at Sudbury and the Blackhorse at Winchester were the
reassembly points for the men of Concord and Lexington after the battle. And Fraunces Tavern, still standing on the corner of Broad and Pearl Streets in New
York, brings fancies to every lover of things Early
American, of Washington shaking hands with that
memorable group of his officers.

Some idea of the number of inns that dotted our
highways can be obtained from the records of the old
Mohawk Turnpike. The first sixteen miles of it, from
Albany to Schenectady, was built between 1795 and
1800 and this was immediately extended sixty-eight
miles to Utica. Exactly fifty-two taverns are known to
have been on the first fifty miles of this road. But they
were needed because twelve hundred sleighs were
counted going westward on this turnpike in three days,
all packed with families and their goods heading for
western New York and the Ohio country.

There were twelve tollgates between Utica and
Schenectady and it is interesting to note that the gates
introduced here were the portcullis type that lifted up
to allow the toll-payer to pass. Over most of the turnpikes the gate used was simply a turnstile formed by
an equal-armed cross turning on a post in the roadway.
Frequently each arm of the cross was tipped with an
iron point and some nameless soul saw a resemblance
in the arm of the turnstile to the ancient weapon, the
pike, and referred to it as a turnpike. The term caught

on and to this day we call almost any toll road a turn-pike.

Every tollgate, of course, had a list of rates which the passer would be expected to pay. These are interesting, not only for the rates themselves, but also for the indication they give us of the number and variety and the nature of the users.

	Cents		
Sheep, per score	8	Four Horse wagons	
Hogs " "	8	tires under 6 inches	75
Cattle " "	18	Five Horse wagons	
Horses " "	18	tires under 6 inches	87½
Mules " "	18	Six Horse wagons	
Horse and rider	5	tires under 6 inches	100
Tied Horses, each	5	One Horse Cart	6
Sulkies	12½	Two Ox Cart	6
Chairs	12½	Three Ox Cart	8
Chariots	25	Four Ox Cart	10
Coaches	25	Six Ox Cart	14
Coachers	25	One Horse Sleigh	6
Phaetons	25	Two horse or Ox Sleigh	6
Two Horse Stages	12½	Three horse or Ox Sleigh	8
Four Horse Stages	18½	Four horse or Ox Sleigh	10
One Horse wagons	9	Five horse or Ox Sleigh	12
Two Horse wagons	12½	Six horse or Ox Sleigh	14
Three Horse wagons	15½		

They seem to have taken care of all the possibilities except the pedestrian, and at prices that returned as much as 20 per cent profit to the stockholders.

Many people resented these high rates and stories are told of the ways they showed their resentment— one of them scribbled these two lines on some paper and left it to greet the tollkeeper when he appeared on the job in the morning.

*"The man who stopped the boy when going to the mill,
Will find his gate at the bottom of the hill."*

Beyond any doubt even the meanest of the taverns was a welcome sight to the weary traveler after some twelve to fourteen hours on the road. In fine weather a couple of hours on the road could be pleasant enough; you would have time really to look at the scenery as you jogged along the highway, but as the day wore on and you swallowed more and more dust and the sun beat down on you without mercy it must have become almost unbearable. Therefore when you pulled up in front of an inn where you knew you could put some water on your face and get some of the dust out of your throat and some food in your stomach, any place would look good. The problem of a dusty road is virtually unknown to any of us now; our roads are all concrete or asphalt with virtually no trace of dust under any conditions. But in the days of which we are speaking the dust lay many inches deep on every traveled highway, stirred by every vehicle and horse. If no wind was blowing the dust lay in a thick blanket over the roadway, so thick that it was at times hard for the driver to see the side of the road, while if the wind was blowing it was even worse as the dust was blown forcibly into the mouth and eyes—there was no escape from it. If you were passing through rolling country where today you can see the road winding a couple of miles ahead of and behind you, like a white ribbon between fields of green, in those early days you would see behind you only a swirling streak of yellow dust from the bed of the road thirty feet or so into the air marking every foot of your pathway.

In rainy weather the problem of dust was temporarily solved only to be replaced with deep, wet, sticky mud. The wheels of the wagon would cut down into the mud and the sticky stuff would curl over the rims of the wheels and move up the spokes until they were hub-deep—the floor of the wagon being the final stopping point. Then the wagon would have to be unloaded, emptied of both passengers and goods; some of the men would have long rails, either carried for the purpose or borrowed from the roadside, to pry the wheels out while others urged the struggling horses to do their best.

A Reverend Mr. Read, traveling through Ohio, has left us a few lines describing his trip. As you read them you are conscious of the ministerial restraint he was using in his choice of words. The year was 1834 and he was taking the fine new stagecoach over an equally

new turnpike from Sandusky to Columbus. He seems
to have spent a stormy night in an inn in Sandusky
where he had heard more swearing than he had ever
believed possible. Long before daylight he was told
to get aboard. He found that he was to be the only
passenger and he rather looked forward to getting
away from the noisy inn and its rough crowd. But the
glass in the doors of the coach was broken and the
rain had soaked the seats and left a puddle on the floor
as the mud had stopped up the drain holes. The wind
blew the curtains in his face and the soaked upholstery
was gradually wetting the seat of his trousers. "All
that had been intimated about bad roads now came
upon me," he wrote. "They were not only bad, they
were intolerable; they were rather like a stony ditch
than a road. The horses on the first stages could only
walk most of the way; we were frequently in up to
the axle-tree, and I had no sooner recovered from a
terrible plunge on one side than there came another in
the opposite direction. I was literally thrown about
like a ball. Let me dismiss the subject of bad roads for
this journey by stating, in illustration, that with an
empty coach and four horses, we were seven hours in
going twenty-three miles . . . Yet this line of conveyance was advertised as a 'splendid line, equal to any
in the states.' "

During the entire nineteenth century the old reliable
cry of the politician, the one argument that he could
champion without fear of opposition from his bitterest
enemy, was, "Get the farmer out of the mud." Everybody talked about the problem and not a few tried to
do something about it, but it was not to be solved until
the twentieth century brought the automobile. Some
roads were built by laying six-inch logs side by side in
the mud—corduroy roads they were called. The wash-
board surface transmitted a vibration to the passengers
that kept them constantly shaking. Lumber was supposed to be inexhaustible, so roads were built of miles
and miles of heavy planks three inches thick and a foot
wide laid on four-by-four sleepers which, in turn, were
laid directly on the ground. Fine for a year or two;
long enough for the toll road-builder to pay his first

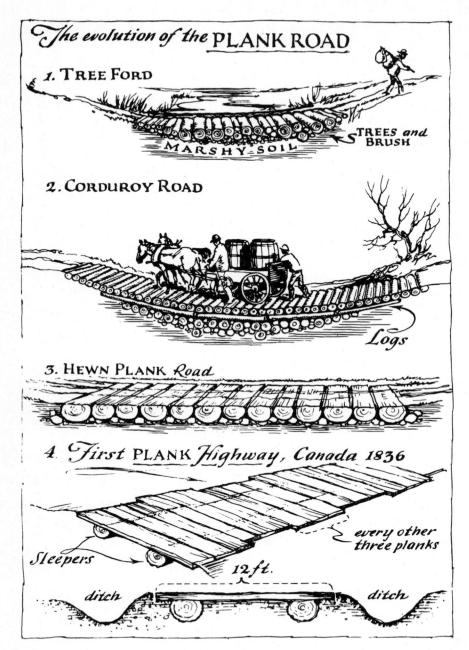

Eric Sloan's OUR VANISHING LANDSCAPE, published by Wilfred Funk, Inc.

dividends, then they would begin to wear out and work loose and the gaping holes would make travel in the mud and dust once more the order of the day. In the winter conditions were somewhat better. If you had runners for your wagon and the snow was deep enough—but not too deep—you could get along a highway rather easily. For this reason outlying farmers tried to plan their delivery of certain crops to the market when the snow made it practical. But with the coming of spring and the warming suns of April when, to the poet, all life would come into its own, the farmer found it was just the opposite. He was tied to his farm just as irrevocably as if he were on an island in the middle of an ocean. The roads were a sea of mud that was deep, dark, and bottomless.

In the rainy seasons the peddler was almost the only traveler with the courage to attempt the roads, and then only if he had wide tires on his wagon. They would not sink so quickly into the mire as narrow wheels, but once they had dug their way in a foot or more it took a powerful horse to pull the wagon out. Wheels had been invented on which the spokes slanted outward instead of vertically, but they seemed to be of little use, and disc wheels apparently were never tried.

With so many thousands of people on the roads carrying all of their worldly goods with them, it might be supposed that the highways of early America would have been beset by gangs of thieves preying on the helpless, and to some extent this was true. But if we are to believe the records, our highways were far freer of road agents than those of England in the same period. For a reason that is not thoroughly understandable now, most American emigrants heading for the back country had a habit of carrying the bulk of their cash in the form of bank drafts and negotiable paper of one kind and another, while the Englishman loved his gold.

However, we had some minor offenders: for example there was the peddler who had sold out his stock of goods and was making his way rather leisurely back to Hartford. He had even sold out all the things he had taken in place of cash and had a pockful of greenbacks. He had taken a fancy to the proprietor of an inn in the Buffalo area, and instead of driving on the next morning he lingered a day or two longer, running up quite a tab in the taproom. He had taken note of a fine black horse the innkeeper kept in a pasture some distance back of the inn and after lunch he strolled out to get a better look at the animal. Others might call it temptation but not the peddler; to him it was nothing short of inspiration. Down the road he led the horse for a mile or two, stopped at a farm, sold him for cash, and walked back to the inn in time for dinner.

Having noted where the new owner would keep the horse he walked over very early next morning, grabbed the bridle and led him by a back route down the road a couple of miles where, as luck would have it, he found another farmer in need of a fine black horse. The deal was soon made and back to the inn he went.

The innkeeper was particularly gracious to him that evening, buying him a couple of steaming hot toddies before dinner and telling him a good story, and as a consequence his conscience began to bother him. But a pony of brandy with his apple pie showed him the way out of his trouble. He walked quietly down to the new home of the horse (who by this time was getting used to it) rode him bareback through the woods to the pasture of the inn where he left him; the horse had not yet been missed. In the morning he paid his bill in full and with the best wishes of the innkeeper resumed his journey to Hartford.

———◆———

TAVERN SIGNS

In the early years of the nineteenth century the ability to read was not nearly as common as it is now. Moreover, naming the streets and numbering the houses was still not common practice. Yet the proprietor of a business had to have some way to impress the nature of his business and his location on the local citizens. Of course the same situation existed in England: a shoemaker called attention to his place of business with a black boot carved out of wood swinging

in front of his shop. The chemist would have a mortar and pestle while the barber used the ancient striped pole reminiscent of the day when he practiced minor surgery between haircuts.

Our tavernkeepers naturally tended to follow the customs of the English and so the visitor from England might find a more or less exact replica of his favorite London tavern in Philadelphia or Boston. But by no means were all of our tavern signs copies of those in Europe; for example the Spread Eagle in Boston clearly showed its American origin in the use of the eagle, though in this particular case the quality of the art work on the sign seems to have left doubts in the minds of many as to what the bird was: the place was for years known as the Broiled Chicken.

The wide use of signboards furnished employment to a great many itinerant artists, including a few who were to become well-known artists later on. In England some of these great ones, such as Hogarth, would undertake to paint a sign on a dare or to win a bet over a glass of rum. Richard Wilson painted the Three Loggerheads for a tavern in Wales, while George Morland is said to have painted signs for the Goat in Boots, the White Lion, and the Cricketers.

Frequently the picture was accompanied by a verse if someone could be found to compose one. Ibbetson is supposed to have paid his bill at an inn on his return from a fishing trip by painting two faces, one decidedly flushed and the other one pale, adding the following verse:

> *Thou mortal man that livest by bread,*
> *What makes thy face to look so red?*
> *Thou silly fop that looks so pale,*
> *Tis red with Tommy Burkett's ale.*

Although the names of English taverns were brought over here, and many early American taverns bore them, there was a difference in accent between the English of England and the American dialect, and many of the original names took on new forms. Thus, the American inn the Cat and Wheel has been definitely traced to the Catherine Wheel in London; this in turn came from St. Catherine's wheel, a reference to the manner in which the saint was martyred. The Goat and Compass over here derived undoubtedly from the old motto "God Encompasseth Us." You can barely recognize the Bacchanalian in the tavern name to which it was unconsciously downgraded over here: the Bag o' Nails. The Pig and Carrot could be easily painted on a sign and recognized by an American; actually it seems to have come from Paris, where it was Pique et Carreau—which in French means simply the spade and diamond of playing cards. Addison has left us some remarks about the Bell Savage, a tavern name fairly common in England; it was usually illustrated with a picture of an Indian standing beside a bell. Said Addison, "I was formerly very much puzzled upon the conceit of it; till I accidentally fell into the reading of an old romance translated out of the French, which gives an account of a very beautiful woman who was found in a wilderness, and is called in French 'La Belle Sauvage' but is everywhere translated by our countrymen as 'The Bell Savage.' "

The Bull and Mouth swinging over the door of a tavern seems to make some sort of crude sense, but it takes a long distance telescope to see its origin, the Battle of Boulougne Mouth (or harbor), fought back in the days of Henry VIII.

Benjamin West, when he was an itinerant artist, must have spent a great deal of his time and talents on sign painting in his younger days. No less than a dozen signs in the Philadelphia area are credited to him. All of these are now either in museums or in private collections. However the authenticity of some of them may be questionable.

Every war brings about some quick changes in some of our habits and ways of thinking, and the signs that the taverns used to entice the tippler were no exception. After Wolfe's victory at Quebec a rash of Wolfe taverns appeared everywhere, and this included one owned by General Israel Putnam in Connecticut. The Declaration of Independence caused at least a few changes, as of course if a sign was too unmistakably

English, down it would come or it would be used for target practice. The King's Head in both Boston and New York disappeared over night, along with the King's Arms and even St. George and the Dragon, and in their places appeared the Washington Tavern or some variations of the name. The patriots of the day had no objection to a little flag-waving if we can judge by the circular published in 1816 by James Carson, proprietor of the Washington Inn at Holmesburg, Pennsylvania:

"Ye good and virtuous Americans—come! whether business or pleasure be your object—call and be refreshed at the sign of Washington. Here money and merit will secure you respect and honor, and a hearty welcome to choice liquors and to sumptuous fare. Is it cold? You shall find a comfortable fire. Is it warm? Sweet repose under a cool and grassy shade. In short, every exertion shall be made to grace the sign of the hero and statesman who was first in war, first in peace and first in the hearts of his countrymen.

In Frankford, Pennsylvania, the Beehive Tavern held forth for many years, its sign showing not only a beehive, but also a bit of poetry:

> *Here in this hive we're all alive,*
> *Good liquor makes us funny.*
> *If you are dry, step in and try*
> *The flavor of our honey.*

Philadelphia may have had rather more originality about its tavern signs than other parts of the country; for example, one William McDermott owned a place at what is now Thirteenth and Locust Streets and this verse invited the thirsty citizens of the day to come in

> *I William McDermott lives here,*
> *I sells good porter, ale, and beer,*
> *I've made my sign a little wider*
> *To let you know I sell good cider.*

Down on the docks in Philadelphia, or in fact in any of our ports, rhymes such as the following were common:

Coil up your ropes and anchor here,
Till better weather does appear.

Philadelphia had another place that came to be known around town as the Four Alls because of its sign. The sign showed the picture of a king on the steps of his palace, an officer in uniform, a clergyman in gown, and a laborer in working clothes. The inscription below read—

> *King—I govern ALL.*
> *General—I fight for ALL.*
> *Minister—I pray for ALL.*
> *Laborer—And I pay for ALL.*

Shortly after the Revolution someone in Boston opened a tavern called A Good Woman and the sign was a painting of a woman minus any head. This was soon copied by others with such variations as the Quiet Woman and the Silent Woman. All of these may have stemmed from a London sign in the time of Henry VIII in which Henry was shown on one side of the sign and a picture of an ordinary woman on the reverse side over the title "A Good Woman"—a reference to Anne Boleyn.

Not only innkeepers but other tradesmen used illustrated signs and verses. One example is a sign that appeared on a blacksmith's shop which is typical. A reproduction of it can be seen over the shop of the Blacksmith in Williamsburg, Virginia, today. It seems that the Colonial blacksmiths had an audience in those days, just as they did when Longfellow wrote the lines

> *And children coming home from school*
> *Look in at the open door;*
> *They love to see the flaming forge,*
> *And hear the bellows roar,*

For he wrote,

> *Who stoppeth here my work to view*
> *Must guard his child and good wife too*

*The Smith must strike while iron is hot
And know which is and which is not.*

LIFE IN
THE INNS
AND
TAVERNS

The familiar signs of the taverns, and their lights burning cheerily in the dusk, were a welcome sight to the weary peddler, whether he came on horseback or in his own wagon or by stage. He could look forward to having a couple of toddies in the taproom and backing up to the blazing fire to warm the bite of the winds out of his aching legs. He would have a chance to chat with a group of roistering emigrants or half a dozen other peddlers from New England and even a scattering of local people who found that an evening at the inn with strangers brought a dash of excitement into their dreary, isolated lives.

A peddler's welcome at an inn was not always unqualified, as witness a sign that hung in the Buckthorn Tavern that stood for many years in New York:

*Four pence a night for a bed
Six pence with supper
No more than five to sleep in one bed
No boots to be worn in bed
Organ grinders to sleep in the wash house
No dogs allowed upstairs
No beer allowed in the kitchen
No Razor grinders or Tinkers taken in.*

We can be sure that the hardworking innkeeper that had this sign made for the information of would-be guests had no idea of being funny. He must have had some bad experiences with peddlers, particularly with the kind that sold some kind of service instead of merchandise. The fact that he would allow the organ grinders at least to sleep in the wash house while he excluded the razor grinders entirely must be taken as a tribute to music.

However, innkeepers who barred peddlers were the exception. To have done so would have been almost fatal to their business, as the army of peddlers far outnumbered any other one group of travelers.

The Hartford Atheneum has in its possession a sort of log book in which the proprietor of Wadsworth Tavern of that city meticulously attempted to enter the name and the business of each guest. The entries between August 1, 1820, and March 24 of the following spring, when he apparently gave it up for lack of time, show that 147 of his guests were peddlers.

Of course in those days virtually everyone paid the peddler in merchandise instead of cash and accordingly the peddler paid the innkeeper in goods. In fact when anyone started on a trip that was going to require an overnight stop somewhere the usual thing was to carry along a quantity of goods of some kind that would be exchangeable at the inn for its hospitality. Almost any thing in common use would do, such as a pound or two of "perlash" (this was the alkaline mixture, obtained by running water through wood ashes, out of which soap was made) or a bundle of raw wool or flax and any staple food such as salt pork or dried beans. At the end of a busy day an innkeeper's "cash register" must have resembled a modern rummage sale.

The roadside inn of the early nineteenth century served every purpose of the modern hotel, except, of course, that it functioned on a much smaller scale and had fewer amenities. While a great part of its custom was with travelers, people who lived near by also patronized it; it was a social center of sorts for both natives and those from far away.

The landlord whose inn was a staging stop, for changing horses and feeding hungry passengers who would then hurry on to the next inn, had an advantage over other innkeepers in that his place would be busy all day, as stages full of passengers arrived at regular intervals, or for an all-night stay if it was late in the evening. The number of stage lines had increased so much by the 1830's that no one inn in a traveled area could take care of them all, and consequently as many as half a dozen taverns within a radius of a mile or two might all be staging inns.

As competition to cut down traveling time grew between the stage companies, every driver would do his best to keep going at top speed. While they were still a mile or so away from the inn the drivers would blow their horns loud and long, in the hope that the landlord would have fresh horses ready to slip into harness so they could be on their way.

For overnight guests the inn provided only two sleeping rooms—one for the ladies and one for the men. Ladies very seldom traveled alone, for a lady alone was an object of suspicion; something must be wrong, or she would have a husband or a relative or a respectable female companion with her.

Accommodations were fairly primitive, and while in the winter the large inn room with its blazing fire must have given everything the appearance of comfort and cheer, in summer it must have been intolerable. Air conditioning was, of course, non-existent, and electric fans were far in the future; and—worst of all—screens for doors or windows were unheard of, so that flies and mosquitoes and all the insects around had free access to the house. Common wire screen was not invented until about 1880 and it was long after that that its use became widespread. And so flies abounded and the public was apparently indifferent to them. There was an old wives' tale that "flies were supposed to be good for you," but I suspect it was invented in desperation because there was really nothing that could be done about them.

One story that indicates the prevalence of flies, and

The bar room in the Wayside Inn, South Sudbury, Massachusetts. *New York Public Library.*

people's attitude toward them, has come down to us. One peddler was a little more fastidious than his fellows. He sat in the common dining room of the inn trying his best to eat his dinner before the flies consumed both it and him. He finally gave up in disgust and walked out into the taproom to find the proprietor to ask him if something could be done to drive the flies away. The honest answer of the innkeeper showed genuine understanding and sympathy. "Oh, yes," he said, "they are something awful in the dining room in the evening, but when you eat breakfast there, nary a fly will you find—they are all in the 'necessary,' so it ain't so bad."

In addition to the common rooms, sleeping rooms, and the "necessary," every inn had its taproom, the real social center for guests and passers-by, where our hardy ancestors consumed drinks that have become famous and often survived to this day in modified form.

In Colonial days they served cider, beer, and ale, with some wine except in the Dutch-settled areas where in addition to beer and ale they favored schnapps (Holland gin). But as we have seen, rum took over in the early 1700's and spread from New England all over the country. Bourbon whiskey is of course an American product, originating in the regions we now call the Middle West and South.

The Washington administration had imposed a tax at the source on domestic liquor in the early 1790's, resulting in what we now call the Whiskey Rebellion. Soldiers were sent into western Pennsylvania and put down the rebellion, but Congress removed the tax almost immediately and domestic liquor remained tax-free until 1862, when the government imposed the first of a long line of taxes to be saddled on the distiller. Bourbon whiskey or "corn likker" competed directly with rum from New England, bourbon being even cheaper than rum, which could be had for a few cents a quart.

Rum was consumed in a vast number of mixtures under a great many different names, one of the most popular being "flip." In the old *New England Almanac* of December, 1704, we read:

The days are short, the weather's cold,
By tavern fires tales are told.
Some ask for dram when first come in,
Others with flip and bounce begin.

Flip was made in a large earthenware pitcher; the pitcher was filled about two thirds full of strong beer sweetened with sugar or molasses. Then a quantity of rum was added (the amount is not specified, it being assumed that the mixer would use his own judgment). Then the loggerhead, always ready in the fireplace, would be used to stir the contents for a full minute. The loggerhead was an iron poker eight to ten inches long. Several of them were essential equipment in any fireplace in a tavern, where they were kept ready and almost red hot at all times. Stirring the mixture with this hot iron of course would cause the liquid to foam and froth and at the same time give it a bitter, burnt taste that was dearly loved by our ancestors. I have never tried this drink, but I am told by friends who have that it is not so good, that the tastes of those old timers must have been different from ours.

As for the loggerheads, you may still find them in

antique stores since they are almost indestructible. They could be used as a club if nothing better was at hand; consequently they were always handy when an argument before the fireplace reached the stage where one or both of the contestants would start looking for something to drive home his point—hence our term "at loggerheads."

Under the name of punch our hardy ancestors swallowed prodigious quantities of liquor. The name was brought to us by sailors from India in the late 1600's. The Hindustani word *panch* referred to the five ingredients that went into it. Of course American inventiveness immediately starting making improvements in it and I believe the final experiment has not yet been reached. Almost as essential as the ingredients was the vessel it was served in. For some reason punch was served in bowls in the early 1700's (I mean individual bowls), and only a little later the huge bowl with its numerous attendant mugs became customary.

Punches were named for persons, for places, for taverns and hosts, for bartenders and stage drivers and celebrities. We think of the various citrus juices as being quite modern but here is an advertisement from the Salem (Massachusetts) *Gazette* of 1741:

"Extraordinary good and very fresh Orange juice which some of the very best punch tasters prefer to Lemmon, at one dollar a gallon. Also very good lime juice to put into punch. . . .

The original five ingredients climbed to a number that was almost astronomical but the one essential continued to be rum. It reminds me of the precautions which Earle mentions in *Stage Coach and Tavern Days*, published in 1900. An old Irishman was apparently watching a landlord mixing a bowl of punch for him.

"Shtop shtop ye are not commincin right and in due ordher. Ye musthn't iver put your whiskey or rum foorst in your punchbowl and thin add wather; for if ye do, ivery drop of wather ye put in is just cruel spoilin of the punch; but foorst—put some wather in bowl— some, I say, since in conscience we must—*thin* pour in the rum; and sure ye can aisly parcaive that ivery dhrop ye put in is afther makin the punch betther and betther."

The landlord, who generally held forth in the taproom, was usually a stable member of the community. Though not a farmer himself, in the sense that he did not work at farm labor, his inn was almost always part of a fair-sized farm where he could raise the fruits, vegetables, and other foods that he served at his table.

Landlords as a class had the reputation of being incorrigibly curious, forever prying into a guest's business, often to the point of exasperation. This was natural enough in a businessman, for he would want to know that he would be paid and that he was not harboring a criminal or other undesirable character. Benjamin Franklin is said to have become so annoyed at the curiosity of landlords that he formulated a standard greeting, which he always used on entering an inn, to save himself time and energy. He would say, "My name is Benjamin Franklin. I was born in Boston. I am a printer by profession, am traveling to Philadelphia, shall have to return at such and such a time, and have no news. Now what can you give me for dinner?"

By and large, the landlord was a fairly upright citizen, if we allow for an occasional scamp, such as can be found in any profession. One landlord acquired the reputation of tricking the passengers who stopped for a single meal by having the driver call out, "Stage is ready" before they could possibly eat the dinner they had ordered and paid for. However a peddler chose to disregard the hasty summons, leisurely eating his dinner while the stage drove off without him. Finishing the roast he called for a bowl of custard for dessert. Not a spoon could be found on the table to eat it with, although there had been plenty of them when the stage had stopped. The peddler called the landlord and demanded spoons, at the same time asking him if he thought that that stageful of people were all fools; were they going to go on their way without getting something for their money? In fact he could easily point out the very man that took those spoons. The furious landlord quickly had a stable boy saddle one of his best horses and go after the stagecoach. After a whispered explanation, the driver turned the stage around and returned to the inn in spite of the complaints of the passengers. The excited innkeeper rushed out to the stage, dragging the peddler with him and saying, "Now you just p'int out the man that took them spoons." "Sure thing, Squire," said the peddler, as he climbed into the best seat in the coach, "I'll p'int him out. I took 'em myself. You will find every one of them in the big coffeepot on the table. C'mon, driver, let's be going."

Years later, and so far away from the scene of this incident that it is hard to imagine there being any connection, something similar happened. Grant Thorburn gives the story. "At the tavern, dinner was ready, but there was no contract for time to eat; after grace by Dr. Cox (too long for the occasion) we begun to eat. Scarcely had I swallowed half my first course when in came the driver hallowing 'All ready.' I thought there was a stable-yard understanding between him and the landlord, for while we were brushing the dust from our clothes, mustering and saying grace, he was eating and drinking as fast as he could, and I did not observe that he paid anything." Thorburn adds that he suspected the parson was a party to the "stable-yard understanding."

Thus the needs of the peddlers created the roads, for which new coaches were developed, which in turn led to the stagecoach and tavern era. In the far West, coaches and some kind of tavern continued in use throughout the century; but in the East the character of travel was to change drastically with the coming of the railroads in the 1840's and 1850's. Public interest switched to railways and road-building came to an almost complete stop. At one time, between Charleston, South Carolina, and Augusta, Georgia, three stagecoaches a week made the trip each way, carrying a total of a little over fifty passengers a month. When a rail line was built and had been in operation for a full year it was carrying nearly 16,000 passengers in a period of only six months.

But while it flourished, the stagecoach-and-tavern system of travel served the peddler well and helped to push the frontiers of commerce further into the continent.

PART II

WHAT THE PEDDLERS SOLD:
THE ORIGIN OF
EARLY AMERICAN ANTIQUES

6

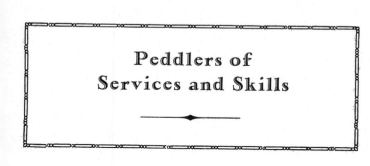

Peddlers of
Services and Skills

With the development of transportation and the extension of the frontiers into the wilderness, many kinds of peddlers took to the roads, not all of them carrying wares. Some had special skills; they might set out on their travels with nothing but their brains and their tools and later leave behind them objects which we now cherish as Early American antiques. Others merely sold services—for example, repairs to household articles, carpentry, cobbling.

In places where there were no established retail stores or services, business depended almost entirely on itinerants; and as they increased in number and variety it became impossible to classify them all as purveyors of merchandise. What they carried with them, tangible or not, permanent or perishable, became an integral part of our culture.

And so the common laborer and the skilled workman become part of the story of the early American peddlers. Let us see where they came from and how they happened to take to the trails.

During the entire Colonial period, and for some years after, fully 90 per cent of our people depended for a living upon agriculture, either food crops or domestic animals. A thin stream of skilled workmen was coming in from Europe, but there were never nearly enough to make any serious change in our economy. Where common labor was required we had to depend mostly on indentured servants, convicts, or slaves.

The fact that large numbers of slaves came in is well known, but the fact that we also absorbed large numbers of convicts is not nearly so well known. The word "convict" has an ominous sound to us; we probably picture him as a beetle-browed murderer ready to kill at the drop of a hat. But in Colonial times we must remember that in England fully two hundred "crimes" were punishable by death (not just one or two as it is now); as a consequence, to be banished to America at that time could result from a very trifling offense. However, between 1717 and the opening of the Revolution, no less than 40,000 convicts were absorbed into our middle Atlantic and southern colonies. Maryland had to take 500 a year from 1750 up to the Revolution, a total of about 13,000 for that colony alone. So come they did; contractors were paid only five pounds per man F.O.B. London.

Indentured servants were different in that their only misdemeanor was not having enough money to pay their passage over here. They simply presented themselves to a ship's captain in any English port, explained the circumstances, and if they were able even to walk they were accepted and brought over. On arrival here they were sold to the highest bidder and the price usually ran between two and four pounds per person in the case of a young man who was strong and healthy, with top prices being paid if he had some particular skill.

A Philadelphia newspaper dated as late as 1817 carried the following advertisement:

THE PASSENGERS

On board the brig Bubona, from Amsterdam, and who are willing to engage themselves for a limited time, to defray the expenses of their passage, consist of persons of the following occupations, besides women and children, viz: 13 Farmers, 2 Bakers, 2 Butchers, 8 Weavers, 3 Tailors, 1 Gardner, 3 Masons, 1 Mill-sawyer, 1 White-smith, 2 Shoemakers, 3 Cabinet makers, 1 Coal burner, 1 Barber, 1 Carpenter, 1 Stocking weaver, 1 Cooper, 1 Wheelright, 1 Brewer, 1 Locksmith.

Apply on board of the Bubona, opposite Callowhill-street, in the river
Delaware, or to W. Odlin & Co. 38 South Wharves.

About the only practical difference between being
an indentured servant and a slave was that the indentured person would remain "sold" only for a limited
time. This ranged from five years to as high as seven,
but at the end of that time the master had to give the
indentured man two suits of clothes, the tools of his
trade, and a small sum of money. The treatment received by the indentured servant depended entirely on
the character of the man who bought him. The master
could work him to death if he wanted to, reasoning that
he was going to have to give him up at the end of the
period anyway so that it did not matter if the man was
by then nearly worn out. On the other hand an out-and-
out slave was like a horse: if you did not feed and care
for him he would depreciate in value and you might
want to sell him later on.

But once his term was up the indentured man (or
woman) was free to go wherever he chose. In the
middle Atlantic colonies, where labor had a more respected status than in the south, he was free to open
up a shop or take to the road as a peddler or as a
skilled itinerant workman.

During all this period the New England colonies
and Virginia managed somehow to avoid taking in any
significant number of these indentured servants, a fact
that the people of those states still like to tell you. This
attitude was reflected for a great many years after 1820,
when the whole business of indenture came to an end,
in the common use of the expressions "hired man" or
"hired girl" throughout not only New England but
those parts of the Middle West which were settled by
New Englanders. Somehow it had a better sound to
the ear than any kind of "servant" did.

Most of the stories of all this temporary slavery
that have come down to us are sad, as might be expected, but at least one of them is really funny. An
Irishman landed at Philadelphia, where he was quickly
bought by a somewhat dull-witted farmer from the
interior. They set out on horseback for the farm, which

was about three days' ride from the pier. The first night they put up at an inn, rolling up in blankets and sleeping on the floor along with all the other guests. The Irishman smelled opportunity, however: he got up at the break of day, woke the landlord, gave him a story that he had paid a lot more money for "this fellow" than he felt now that he could afford, and he was willing to let him go for half the sum he was worth. He went on to tell the landlord that the fellow talked as though he really knew how to grow fine vegetables and fruit, and you could see how young and strong he was. In fact, so far as he could see, the fellow had only one bad habit and that was "lying." He was given to telling lies about himself, but they did harm to nobody. Of course the landlord bought, and we can picture the scene when he woke the farmer up to have him start his day's work—the new arrival from Erin being well on his way along the highway.

APPRENTICES

Another source of at least semiskilled labor was the apprentice system. While it never seems to have been carried out here as strictly as it always had been in England, where a young man bound himself out to a tradesman for a period of years to learn the trade, it did make some approach to it. After a period of years the young man was free to go where he liked. He was provided with the tools of the trade he had learned and he was now known as a "journeyman" because he was expected to travel from place to place in the practice of his trade.

Opportunity beckoned from inland rather than from the more settled port cities. A settler could not have great skill or experience in *all* of the trades whose products he would require. A pioneer's wife could spin, weave, and dye her wool or flax into cloth, but she might be unable to tailor a suit of clothes. So if a young man knocked on the door and announced that he was a tailor, he was apt to be invited in and an arrangement made to feed and house him while he made the suit. He would carry with him an assortment of needles and pins, buttons and thread; and in less than a week the master of the house would find himself the owner of a new suit or overcoat of homespun that might be expected to last him many a year. Down South the going for an itinerant tailor was nowhere nearly as good as it was in the Middle West. If you were a "gentleman" in the South you had a tailor in London who had your measurements. You also had your cotton importer in London who took your crop each year. Thus by devious interchanges the gentleman had his suits made in London, the tailor collected from the cotton importer, and shipped the new clothing to America. In theory this worked out fine, but we are told that a hitch in the chain frequently occurred so that a man got the wrong suit.

But in the North the itinerant tailor made out well for many years. Soon, instead of trudging along on foot, he was able to buy a horse, and with that advantage he could carry along a few yards of cloth that he had picked up at one of the new woolen mills in the East, and thus be able to offer his prospect a real "store suit." Brooks Brothers, well known to many generations of New Yorkers for their clothing, boast that the beginnings of their business was in supplying these traveling tailors with woolen goods.

THE COBBLERS

The cobbler's trade was somewhat similar to the tailor's. In medieval England, when a man's shoes were little more than folds of leather wrapped and tied around his feet, the man would make his own and the whole family's shoes. But in the 1600's a sole was added and shoes were fastened on with a buckle. Samples of early Colonial shoes may be seen in Williamsburg in Virginia today. You may be startled when you first look at them, wondering just why they look so different from today's shoes. But in a moment you realize that both shoes are identical—no left and right—and the toes inclined to be much squarer than on the shoes we wear today.

After the Revolution the journeyman shoemaker took to the trails west and south: at first he might carry only his lapstone, hammer, knives, and pegs all

The cobblers' bench enabled the shoemaker to sit in comfort while he worked. *New York Public Library.*

wrapped in his leather apron and hung over his shoulder. If he was working in the South where the wives of the big plantation owners affected the new French high heels, he would have to carry along a supply of those. They were made of wood just as many of them are today, only at that time they were whittled out by hand. The lady would supply the silk or satin covering for the cobbler to sew and glue tightly to the wooden form.

Of course the shoemaker had to take his pay in whatever medium was prevalent at the time and place. If in the rare event that it was in cash it would be two shillings for each pair of shoes made, plus, of course, board and lodging. But it was much more apt to be in "country pay" which meant, in practice, absolutely anything salable the settler might have on hand. Three pecks of corn were the equivalent of two shillings. In the South the old Spanish silver dollars were common. These were cut in halves and quarters with a chisel and frequently the quarter sections were cut again to make small change, referred to as "bits," more commonly "two bits." In all probability this custom was also the origin of our slang word "chisel."

For many years shoemaking in the country districts was not an all-year-round occupation: in the summer months the demand for farm labor was so great that many of the cobblers were induced to lay aside their lasts and awls to take up the farmer's pitchfork and rake until the harvests were all safely stowed away in the barns and root cellars for the year.

As roads improved to the point where a cart could be driven over them, the shoemakers quickly adopted carts which would not enable them to get around very much faster but did allow them to carry a supply of leathers with them. This was important in the early days, as no matter how badly a farmer might want new shoes they were not possible if tanned leather was not available. The use of a cart had another effect that we still notice today. It enabled the cobbler to bring along his bench, fitted with slots for all of his knives,

Shoemaking tools, *New York Public Library.*

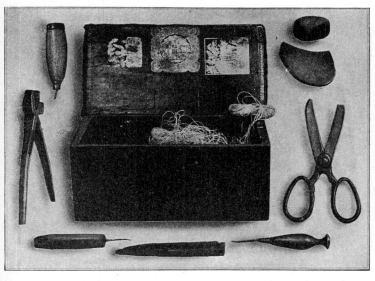
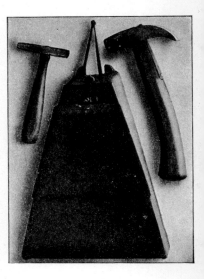

tiny square pockets for nails or pegs and a place for him to sit in comfort while he worked. The cobbler's bench is the product of evolution just as is the palette of the artist and the anvil of the blacksmith. Generations ago it reached such perfection in design that with all our mechanical progress we have not seen fit to make any changes in it. The cobbler's bench is reproduced by the thousands these days, by modern cabinetmakers, to provide an informal note in today's living room. If you are lucky enough to have a genuine old one in good shape you are lucky indeed.

Like all itinerant workmen of the period, who by the nature of their trade became guests in the house for at least a short period, the cobblers systematically carried the news and gossip of the road with them. Undoubtedly this came naturally to many of them, but if it did not they quickly acquired the habit. The housewife expected them to tell about the affairs of all their customers and the man of the house depended upon them for the political news of the countryside. In addition to this function the itinerant would memorize a wide assortment of stories, the bedtime variety for the children and some that were more mature for the adults. In the course of years the open road would begin to lose its fascination for the young journeyman; it might be because of advancing age, but it was more likely to be the attractions of someone's fair daughter. In either event, before long he would open up a permanent shop in the nearest village and cease to be a nomad.

———◆———

THE WEAVERS

The manufacture of fabric from fibers of any and all varieties is a craft that goes so far back in history that its origin is utterly lost. We know that more than five thousand years ago the Egyptians apparently were experts, but where they learned the art may never be known. Certainly the very earliest Colonial wives to arrive here knew how to transform a bundle of wool just sheared from the sheep into a finished piece of woolen cloth. The wool had to be washed and at least some of the grease of the animal taken out of it. Then it had to be carded or combed. This was a matter of combing a bundle of it at a time to get the fibers in line with each other. Then it was ready to be spun into yarn on the spinning wheel, and from the wheel it was brought to the loom where it was woven into cloth. After this stage, if it had not been before, it was put in a bath of dye and then allowed to dry.

The Colonial housewife probably gave a greater portion of her time to these various jobs than to any other one of her duties, for she made the cloth that clothed her whole family.

In the early part of the nineteenth century she was still doing all these things except that now and then she would accept the help of a traveling weaver. Weaving was heavy work even for our sturdy grandmothers. The loom was set up in a corner somewhere, usually in the kitchen, and every time she had a few minutes between other duties she would go over and weave an inch or two.

Up to about 1800, since looms had to be imported, they were apt to be out of the reach of the family in ordinary circumstances. But along with the urge to manufacture everything that we needed, several domestic factories began turning out looms equal to the English-made ones. The peddlers, knowing that huge numbers of these could be sold all over the States, bought them as fast as the factories could turn them out. They sold at about 25 per cent less than the imported looms, so in a short time just about every home in America had one. The dye pot, the spinning wheel, and the loom became standard equipment just as much as the kitchen range, the coffee maker, and the refrigerator are today.

The housewife had a variety of dyes to color her newly made fabric with. If she wanted it brown she used logwood, while she could get a nice turkey red by dipping the cloth in an extract of madder root that she could buy from almost any peddler who came along. However, dyeing is not always an easy job if you want a permanent solid, uniform color and so she developed the habit of using indigo. Indigo produced a good blue, very dark if you left the goods in the bath for some time; but almost any degree of blueness could be obtained. Indigo was as nearly foolproof as any dye could be. It became so popular long before the Revolution that some enterprising planters down in the Carolinas began raising it commercially and shipping it north to New York and Boston where the peddlers picked it up.

It might be hard to prove it now, but the chances are that the main reason why General Washington's army chose blue as the dominant color of our uniforms was the simple fact that indigo was at that time cheap, plentiful, and easy to use.

Naturally the itinerant weaver was turned out of the same mold as his brothers of the road. He made good with his wit and his ready tongue even if not always with his weaving; in fact the weavers as a group acquired a reputation for their never-ending supply of gossip and scandal.

There is something homelike and old-fashioned about a rag rug on the floor of a room furnished in any of the Early American styles—for rugs woven out of rags are truly just as American as ham and eggs or griddlecakes with maple syrup. In the early 1800's they were made mostly by itinerants, weavers who traveled the roads in a cart piled high with rags completely covering a loom that would be as large as he could manage to carry. The weaver would stop at a farm, show the family a sample of his work by spreading a rag rug, kept for the purpose, on the bare floor and then bargain with them. He would use what rags they had, supplement those with some of his own, and then set to work. Usually two or three days would suffice to make a small rug; during that time he would of course be a guest of the family. Many of these old itinerant weavers of rag rugs eventually came to a community that appealed to them and set up a permanent shop in the town, perhaps retaining the cart in order, when necessary, to extend operations farther away. Fairly large numbers of these old rugs are still to be found in the back country; they were made out of every color and kind of cloth that could be found, cotton, linen, wool, and even homespun. The art of weaving rag rugs is still carried on in some parts of the nation.

———◆———

In theory at least the cabinetmaker has about the same relationship to the carpenter that the maker of fine watches has to the men who make the huge clocks we see on public buildings. The dividing line between them is sometimes only the faintest of lines, though sometimes there was a wide gap. It was this way in the Colonial period and it still is today.

Pioneer settlers in a new area were interested initially only in the stark necessities of existence—food, shelter, and clothing. Only when these primary needs became plentiful could they give thought to refinements. Thus when the first English settlers picked a spot on the James River in 1607 they built the easiest and quickest kind of shelters possible with no thought whatever of ornamentation. But when his primary necessities were taken care of and the colonist began to feel that the supply was reasonably certain in the future, *then* he began to look about him to see what might be improved, what he could do to please his eye or his soul.

Physically, practically nothing remains of the homes and furnishings of the earliest arrivals on our shores from Europe, a fact that should not be surprising because they built with only the necessities of the moment in mind, knowing or at least hoping that more satisfying replacements could follow.

And follow they surely did. Years before the first arrivals had reached an advanced age they were building new homes and filling them with professionally made furniture. At first the good furniture was all imported from the mother country, but as early as 1750 cabinetmakers were coming over and setting up shops here. Here they could build a chest or a table or a bed out of native woods and sell it at a price much lower than that of an imported piece. White pine was plentiful and, while it lacked the elegance of mahogany or walnut, it produced pieces of enduring beauty that are valuable antiques today.

The shop and warehouse of Duncan Phyfe on Fulton Street, New York City, c. 1820. *The Metropolitan Museum of Art, Roger's Fund, 1922.*

DUNCAN PHYFE SOFA

By the late eighteenth century in our big eastern cities some people had accumulated enough wealth to allow them to import the work of European masters regardless of cost. But more importantly, we were developing masters in fine cabinet-making ourselves. Duncan Phyfe, in New York, was producing in the very finest cabinet woods furniture that equaled in artistry and design anything from abroad.

But only a few miles inland, unless the settlement was on a river that would allow shipping from the big cities, furniture had to be made locally in the late eighteenth and well on into the nineteenth century.

124

The cycle of necessities first, followed later by the luxuries, repeated itself throughout the Middle West. Journeymen cabinetmakers took to the trails with carts and set out into western New York State, Ohio, Indiana, and south into Kentucky and Tennessee. They carried the simplest of tools with them, not at all the relatively fine equipment that a master craftsman would have at hand.

Some would have a definite settlement in mind when they started out and patiently, week after week, work their way toward it, pausing a few days to repair a farmer's house or make a new table for him, and then on a few more miles with the proceeds of that job. Arriving at the place they had in mind their first thought would be to build a shop. They were all through with traveling. They wished only to settle down and prosper with the community. But we can suppose that the great majority of these workers in wood left the East with no particular destination in mind: they would wander from place to place to the west or to the south until, reaching an appealing community, they built tiny shops for themselves and became respected craftsmen.

We have to bear in mind that in the period after the Revolution and for many years into the nineteenth century the whole idea of a furniture store was entirely unknown. The furniture store of today is strictly the product of the mass production of many furniture factories competing with each other in price and quality for display space in the huge retail outlets. The consumer shops from one display to another until he finds something that at least comes near to what he wanted.

But in the early nineteenth century you went to the shop of the cabinetmaker: he might have two or three pieces made up for you to look at as well as the pieces he was working on at the moment for some other customer, but you told him what you needed and together you worked out the size of each piece and the woods to be used. During the course of the next few weeks he would handcraft every piece you had ordered.

In the big coastal cities of New York, Boston, and Philadelphia the shops of the cabinetmakers employed

DUNCAN PHYFE
CHAIR

as many as a hundred men during this period; but in the small towns three or four men could take care of everything. Power tools, in any modern sense, were of course unknown. Water power might be used where it was available but mostly manual power sufficed: the strong arms of an assistant turning the huge crank of the master's lathe, or the foot treadle that was to operate until the day of steam power.

The early nineteenth century produced an astonishing uniformity in style throughout our small towns and country districts. It lacked the elegance of the master craftsmen of Philadelphia who were trying to imitate and even improve upon the work of Europe. There was no carving and very little turning. But what it lacked in elegance it made up for in the beauty of simplicity. The lines of an Early American piece are as pleasing to many of us today as they were a century and more ago.

Closely allied with the business of the itinerant maker or seller of furniture was one of the most accomplished and famous of early American furniture-makers, Lambert Hitchcock. He was never a peddler himself, but he supplied peddlers with parts of chairs or whole chairs, and they distributed his work to outlying settlements.

Hitchcock was born at Cheshire, Connecticut, in 1795, the son of a Revolutionary soldier who was lost at sea when Lambert was six years old. At an early age he was apprenticed to a cabinetmaker in Litchfield, and served until he was twenty-three. Then, since he wanted to go into business for himself, he sought out a spot where there were few others of his craft, the little town of Barkhamsted in northwestern Connecticut, later called Riverton, and after that Hitchcocksville in his honor. Here, according to Mabel Roberts Moore, historian of the Tercentenary Commission of the State of Connecticut, he built a small turning and framing shop designed to make certain parts of chairs only, such as the turned legs and rungs. These he sold to the peddlers who called at his shop; in turn they either sold them as replacement parts to farm families or, using their own skill, managed somehow to make completed

HITCHCOCK
CHAIR

Hitchcock Chair Factory, Riverton, Connecticut, 1826.

chairs out of them while on the road. The chances are that the peddlers sold most of them as chairs complete except for the seat, and this could be filled in with rush or some combination of cane by the farm housewife.

We know that young Lambert operated this plant from 1818 to 1826, for in 1826 he built what is still used as the Hitchcock chair factory. Now he could make complete chairs, stenciled and finished just as every lover of antique furniture knows them today. He continued to sell as many of these to his peddler friends as he could, but by 1830 his production reached the remarkable level of 15,000 chairs, altogether too many for nearby peddlers to handle. So he began shipping them by wagon to Hartford, where they were loaded onto boats that took them down the Connecticut River to New York. From there shipments were sent down the coast to the various eastern ports. Some of them would be sold to the stores in the port cities, while the balance would be shipped upriver to the trading center at the head of navigation of the river. There they could be sold by the general store, but in all probability most

---

LAMBERT HITCHCOCK,
AGENT,
CHAIR MANUFACTURER,
HITCHCOCKSVILLE, (CONN.)

HAS on hand a large and elegant assortment of Chairs, made after the latest and most approved patterns. *ALSO,* A good assortment of CABINET FURNITURE, all of which he will sell at very low prices.

N B. Two or three Young Men from 16 to 20 years of age, of industrious and correct habits, who will abstain from the use of ardent spirits, can have steady employment as above.

Hitchcocksville, August 17. 1830.   tf 21

---

of them would be sold to the surrounding settlers by the local peddlers working out of the general store. Transportation was still in such wretched condition that the extreme trading area of a general store was a circle not more than five miles in radius.

Lambert Hitchcock's chairs deservedly built a reputation for themselves. They came at a period in our history when only wealthy families in the big cities could afford to import their furniture from England and France, or have it made by one of the two or three master craftsmen we had developed in Philadelphia and New York.

The chairs Lambert Hitchcock made might be considered as a compromise between the classic lines of Sheraton, Hepplewhite, or Empire and the extreme simplicity of Early American. To the inland housewife of that faraway day they were "fancy chairs," the mere possession of which gave her a status far above her neighbors. They were beautiful then and still are today.

———◆———

Originally the tinker was the fellow who was skilled in repairing pewterware. In the cities he went from house to house in search of broken and damaged pewter dishes and spoons which, being soft, got out of shape easily. Inland the tinker was more inclined to go from one town to the next on a horse, with two huge saddle bags filled with his tools and molds so that he was prepared to stay all day with you and repair and polish every piece you had. But as tin- and brassware became more popular he developed skill in repairing things made of those metals too. Thus he became a "handyman," without the specialized skill of a specialist but with enough ability to repair almost any of the simple equipment of the day. I suppose his lineal descendant

THE TINKERS

The tinker repaired and polished pewter, tin and brass household wares. *New York Public Library.*

is the modern "fixit" shop, although the word "tinker" now means to fuss around with some household piece of equipment in a frequently vain effort to avoid calling in a professional.

Some of our early tinkers must have been fairly raffish characters. Edith B. Crumb of the *Detroit News* tells us in *Hobbies Magazine:* "Until the middle of the eighteenth century there were few professional pewterers, but they were itinerants who made a living going about mending pewter spoons and doing a general job of patching and mending of pieces that had melted or cracked. And among these itinerants was one Richard Graves—and what a scamp he must have been —for in 1642 he was arrested once for 'oppression in his trade at pewtering,' a second time for calling his neighbor bad names and a third time when a gentleman testified that 'he heard Rich Graves kissed Goody Gent twice.' When he confessed to the latter he was sentenced to the whipping post and stocks." We do not know what happened to Graves when he recovered from the whipping post and was set free from the stocks. We might assume that if he returned to the practice of his trade he may have ended on the gallows at the rate he was going.

◆

THE GRINDERS

Long before the day of modern abrasives, the product of electric furnaces, tools were sharpened by almost endless rubbing on a piece of natural stone. Nearly any soft, even-grained stone could be made to serve, but here and there around the country nature had left deposits of stone far superior for sharpening tools to the common varieties. Hot Springs, Arkansas, was unusually favored in having two grades still known as Soft Arkansas and Washita. At Berea, Ohio, a deposit of fine-grained sandstone was uncovered in the early 1800's that is still supplying the grindstones of the farmer.

Inevitably the grindstones reached the highway. Maybe a grinder was lucky enough to have acquired one of the really superior stones of the day and to

It required more skill to grind scissors than knives. *New York Public Library*.

have developed more than ordinary skill in its use. But this would be the exceptional case. The usual thing was that, using whatever stone he could get, he rounded it into a wheel, mounted it on a portable stand fitted with a foot treadle and he was in business. He carried a handbell that tinkled continuously as he walked along the road with his apparatus on his back, swinging the bell to announce his presence. Down would go the stand at the signal of a farmer and one by one the farmer would have his axes, his scythes and even the butcher knives from the kitchen put in shape for a few pennies and a little food. In the villages these men were more apt to be known as "scissors grinders," since a pair of shears requires a lot more skill to grind than does a butcher knife.

———◆———

In spite of the fact that the nomadic printers of early America produced at least two immortals, the vast majority of them have to be classed as ne'er-do-wells or tramps with a bit of education. Franklin is the best

PRINTERS
ON THE
ROADS

known of the immortals of course and Mark Twain certainly has a permanent place in the history and folklore of the country.

To be a printer a young fellow had to know how to read and write particularly at a time when such ability was much rarer than it is today. He usually served his time under a master printer and on becoming a journeyman he wandered from town to town. In the first half of the nineteenth century the small-town job printer was quite likely to be the editor of the newspaper as well. So it is easy to reconstruct a fairly common situation. A young journeyman printer comes along wide open to anything that looks like opportunity, calls on the local printer-editor, and since he can set type, if the regular man happens to be too drunk he may be taken on as an assistant to the editor.

Many of these young men remained nomads as long as they lived, acquiring a tremendous range of unrelated experience that could have been highly useful if they had been willing to settle down and take root in one locality. But most of them seemed to prefer staying a few months in one town and then moving on to some place over the horizon.

THE SILHOUETTE CUTTER

For most of the century following the Revolution the only way you could get a likeness of yourself was to call in a portrait-painter or his brother the painter of miniatures, unless you were willing to accept the popular low-priced silhouette.

It seems that in eighteenth century France a newly appointed *controleur generale* instituted so many and such drastic economies that his last name became synonymous with cheapness. So when the outline of one's face, made with a pair of shears and black paper, became popular it was naturally called a silhouette.

During the first half of the 1800's you could expect to meet a silhouette-cutter almost any place people gathered. His equipment consisted of a small pair of very sharp shears and a packet of black paper. The price ranged from fifty cents down to half that sum depending on how hungry the artist was at the moment.

Most of these craftsmen were not itinerants in the sense that they went from house to house, but they did go from one town to another, staying in one place just long enough to skim off most of the business, and then going on to the next town. The introduction of photography sounded the death knell of the art.

———◆———

THE PORTRAIT PAINTER AND THE MURALIST

It has been said that as soon as a people reach the stage where they want to leave behind them likenesses of themselves for their descendants to admire, they are safely past the primitive period. For many of our ancestors this point was reached even before the days of the Revolution. If you were rich enough you might go to England and sit for no less an artist than Sir Joshua Reynolds; but if you were not so affluent you could patronize a native artist who was almost sure to be an itinerant.

The big cities of the East Coast might have one or more painters of established reputation, but inland the painters would have talents ranging from fair down to something a good deal less. Most of them were self-taught and many of the lower fringe would not hesitate to paint tavern signs for their board and keep if nothing better offered.

Benjamin West painted portraits in Philadelphia for some years for the sum of ten guineas each, then went to New York where he was able to double his charges. Copley worked in Boston, New York, and Annapolis, setting up a studio in each place. The records show that in 1771 in New York alone he painted thirty-three portraits and collected fourteen guineas for each of them. Gilbert Stuart worked in New England, New York, and Philadelphia. All of these men were itinerant at least for a time until they could establish themselves in one place.

In the period of the 1700's, when culture was not nearly as widely dispersed as we like to think it is now, an artist could not be very choosy if he wanted to eat regularly. The story is told about one of them, Gustavus

Hesselius, a Swede who traveled through Maryland, Virginia, and Pennsylvania painting portraits when he could get commissions and other things when he could not. He is credited (or blamed) for a great many of the old portraits still to be seen in the three states he covered. He must have been a really handy man because we read that when he was not working with his paint brushes he was installing or repairing church organs. But this did not complete the list of his talents, for we can still read his advertisement in an old copy of the *Pennsylvania Gazette* dated December 11, 1740:

"Painting done in the best manner by Gustavus Hesselius of Stockholm, Coats of Arms drawn on coaches, Chaises etc. or any kind of ornaments, Landscapes, Signs, Shew-Boards, Ship and House painting, gilding of all sorts, writing in Gold or Colour, old pictures cleaned and mended."

And if you think that gentleman's talents were diversified, read the list of accomplishments of Charles Willson Peale of Philadelphia. He was a coachmaker, a silversmith, a saddlemaker, a modeler in wax or plaster. He was also a taxidermist, conducted a private museum, served in the legislature, and was a dentist.

Then there was William Williams who advertised that he "was prepared to paint in general," which must have meant that he would paint anything from a barn to a wash tub. Many other samples of the adaptability of our Colonial ancestors could be given, but I shall end with Peter Pelham who "Paints portraits, engraves, teaches dancing, reading, writing, needlework and painting on glass."

The perambulating artist in the early days seems to have suffered from one of the oldest ills that besets the businessman—the supply of goods far exceeded the demand. Witness the advertisement of one George Mason: "With a view to more constant employment he now draws faces in crayon for two guineas each, glass and frame included."

Then there is the case of Thomas Stuart White in the *New England Weekly Journal* of July 8, 1724. He tells the reader that "unless he meets with sufficient encouragement to oblige him to stay" he will return to England. Unfortunately the records do not tell us what the response to this appeal was.

John Wesley Jarvis lived long before mass production was ever heard of, nevertheless he seemed to have that idea in the back of his head when he set up a portrait factory. His method was to allow each sitter just one hour of his time, during which he would do the man's face; then he would do the face of the next one while his assistant would paint in a custom-made background to suit. Now in the case of Isaac Sheffield of New London we are left to wonder. He seems to have painted mostly sea captains, and a number of the portraits are still around. If you see only one of them you may not be impressed one way or the other, but if you can see two or more of them you are impressed at once with the fact that while the face in each is en-

Mostly self-taught, the itinerant artist often lacked talent. *New York Public Library.*

tirely different, all of the captains are pictured standing in front of the same red curtain and holding the
very same telescope.

Here is another mass-production idea—but this one
had a really ingenious twist to it. Several young artists
would combine their talents, spending a long winter
painting canvases showing heads and shoulders only—
never any faces. Through constant repetition of the
same head and shoulders a painter would acquire both
speed and skill: maybe it was the head and shoulders
of an army officer of the period or a well-dressed gentleman or lady who would have looked at home in the best
drawing room in Philadelphia. Meanwhile the other
painters were grinding out dozens of other heads and
shoulders of important-looking people minus only the
face.

The scheme was really diabolical when you consider
the temptation it must have been when the artist appeared at the door of an isolated farm house with a
bundle of the canvases under his arm. A young man or
woman answers his knock and the artist quickly explains how easy it would be for him to have a genuine
portrait of, say, his father. The chances are that the
father may never have had on a white shirt and a neck-
cloth in his life but with his father's actual face in
the space provided—well what friend in future years
could ever doubt it. And if the father happened to have
been a soldier in the distant past he could become a
major or something higher in rank for the same price.
This was a regular racket during the first half of the
nineteenth century. Naturally no figures are available
on how extensive it became, but we can be sure that at
least a few of the ancestral portraits we see here and
there are exaggerated in this manner.

Painters who attempted murals were very much less
in evidence, although one might think it easier to
paint a scene rather than a human face. Their way of
working must have been to make a sketch of the scene
first and from this paint the actual picture on the wall
or over the mantel. A few samples of their work remain
and when they were done faithfully they have historic

value because they show an authentic scene from the past.

———◆———

In the early part of the nineteenth century, when animal husbandry was showing the first glimmerings of progress from the darkness of superstition, it became a common sight on our back-country roads to see a man driving a great stallion along the road. Sometimes the man would be on foot and sometimes he would be riding the stallion; much later he transported the stallion in a horse-drawn four-wheeled trailer. He would stop at every farmhouse, make suitable inquiries of the farmer, and if the services of his stallion were needed he would bargain with the farmer until a price was reached; this might include board and keep for several days. The price might run between five and ten shillings per service. The owner of an exceptionally fine-looking stallion could make a fair living peddling the services of his animal, and he could work all year 'round if he cared to and did not try to sell more service than nature had provided. The same type of *service* was also peddled by the owner of a fine bull and the price was about the same. Only in the vaguest manner can the need for the services of a particular bull or stallion be said to have been understood at this period. The whole science of veterinary medicine was still in the future.

THE PEDDLER OF SERVICE FOR FARM ANIMALS

———◆———

As in the case of so many itinerants, the peddler who sold a service might also carry the kind of wares he repaired; and this was undoubtedly the case with the gunsmith. He was an important figure in pioneer times. Firearms were vital to the early settler; they were frequently the only means he had of putting meat on his table and protecting his family from hostile Indians or from white men of less-than-honest intentions. Consequently he gave as much care to his firearms as to his home and family; and when his guns needed repairs

THE GUNSMITHS

that he could not make himself the gunsmith was indispensable.

In the Plymouth and Jamestown settlements in the earliest days, firearms were such crude affairs that they probably required no highly skilled repairman. Miles Standish carried a matchlock and John Smith had one like it. A matchlock was fired by applying a lighted match or fuse to a tiny hole in the breech of the gun to ignite the powder which had been poured into the muzzle; the explosion would drive the ball out of the barrel in at least the general direction in which the gun was pointed. The best the user of such a gun could do about aiming it was to carry a crotched stick. When he had to shoot, he would force the stick into the ground, set the gun in the crotch and, if the target was still there, apply the lighted fuse. There was not much to get out of repair. Wheel-lock guns were in existence at the time, but they were more complicated and so expensive that they were seldom used except by wealthy sportsmen.

Sometime in the 1600's a marked improvement in firearms was introduced: it was called the flintlock. The spark was applied to the powder by means of a mechanism in the breech of the gun consisting of a piece of flint and steel activated by a trigger. This gun was used in the eighteenth century and even into the nineteenth. It was superseded when a Philadelphia minister named Forsythe invented what is called a percussion cap. He put a tiny bit of highly explosive chemical into a metal cap, which, when struck by the trigger, went off and propelled the ball. The cap-and-ball gun was a great advance over any previous firearm in common use and lasted until the Civil War.

As firearms became more complicated, repairing them required more specialized skill than the average early settler had, and it also needed uncommon tools; and at this point the gunsmith began to flourish both in settled communities and as a traveler. At first he traveled on horseback, his saddle bags crowded with tools; but you can be sure he adopted a cart or wagon just as soon as he could afford it and the roads would allow him. We know that the traveling gunsmith followed the settlers almost as a man's shadow follows the man. Through the latter part of the eighteenth century and nearly to the end of the nineteenth he wound his way from town to town and from cabin to cabin, highly welcome because of the skill and spare parts that he carried.

For the most part gunsmiths were Germans from the eastern parts of Pennsylvania. From 1750 on a small but very important stream of Germans came over from the Rhineland where they had worked in one of the several munitions factories the technically minded Germans had developed. If they were finished craftsmen they opened a shop in Lancaster or York and made new guns, while if they were not quite so experienced they would take to the highways, well knowing that their services were badly needed.

Several of those that stayed in Bucks County developed a new rifle that later was to become known as the Kentucky rifle all over the Middle West and even into the deep South. It seems to have acquired the Kentucky identification because so many of the pioneers in that area used it in preference to any other. Stories are told that it had a range twice as far as any of the muskets of the period and, even more important, it had such accuracy that you *aimed* it at the target:

Of course the traveling gunsmith carried a stock of

Matchlock, early Colonial period (above) and a typical Kentucky rifle (below). *The American Rifleman.*

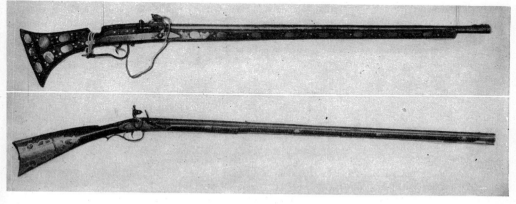

these new guns when he could get them. Many of them were very good-looking as well as efficient, with their long bright barrel inlet into a stock of curly maple with a patch box in shining brass inlaid in the stock. They are choice collectors' items everywhere today in both museums and private collections.

The gun of that period consisted of just three principal parts—the lock, which meant the trigger and hammer mechanism, the long steel barrel, and the wooden stock it rested in. The gun was useless if any one of these parts was out of commission. Arriving at a cabin, the gunsmith learned that the settler's gun had a badly plugged barrel or maybe the stock was so badly split that it could not be held to the shoulder, or it might be part of the lock was missing. In any event the itinerant gunsmith was the welcome answer; he had spare parts that could be skillfully fitted to what was still serviceable or he could sell the settler a *whole new gun*—"lock, stock and barrel."

Such were a few of the peddlers of services, whose functions often overlapped those of the peddler of wares. As our economy expanded and grew more complex, service men might become settled craftsmen, then retail merchants; one man might have a retail establishment from which he sent out peddlers to more remote areas. The evolution of the peddler into the businessman was beginning.

7

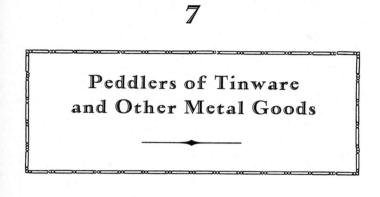

Peddlers of Tinware and Other Metal Goods

For a full century and a half tinware was the number one item carried by the Yankee peddler: whether he carried his stock of goods in a trunk or in a wagon, some items made of tin would always be included.

In the mid-twentieth century, when all of our cooking utensils are made of stainless steel, aluminum, or glass, it is difficult for us to understand the enthusiasm of our ancestors for tinware. But during most of the eighteenth and nineteenth centuries a selection of shiny tinware as a wedding gift would make any bride happy. The bride that could present her husband with a hope chest filled with tin cups and pans, a kettle or two, and maybe even a dishpan could be sure of a delighted reception.

We moderns smile when we read that in Switzerland the status of a farmer among his neighbors is sometimes measured by the size of the manure pile in his front yard; in like manner a wide selection of tinware displayed in the home of one of our early American settlers marked him at once as a man to be reckoned with in the social and economic affairs of the community.

Those of us who can go back in memory to the early part of this century may remember the passing of the old tin cup. Every town or village had its town pump to which was always tied a tin cup. No one, young or old, would pass that pump without stopping for a draught of water from the cool depths of the cup and a moment's chat with a thirsty neighbor. If you were raised on a farm you will hardly have forgotten the pleasure you brought to the men working in the fields when you carried them a pail of cold water from the well and they drank from a tin dipper. And the oil can—I can still remember my mother sending me to the store with the oil can to have it filled with kerosene for the lamps in the house; the grocer would always put a potato over the spout to prevent the contents from sloshing out—never an apple or something I could eat. But the tin cup and the dipper and the oil can have gone into the limbo of the forgotten, superseded by the paper cup and electric lights of our modern times.

Historically tinware is of great interest to the student of early America because out of it our ancestors were able to fashion a vast number of common, everyday things that tell us much about how people lived. These objects were the kind that were scarce or non-existent until tinware was introduced. In Colonial days a family might have one pewter platter for the table and possibly one large bowl and a few spoons. For plates and glasses they would use wooden trenchers and mugs made of rough pottery. If they were among the more fortunate they would have a cast iron pot, hanging by a pothook from the crane, that could be swung in over the fire and then out again when the stew was ready to be heaped onto the trenchers for the hungry family. In the very early days that was about the extent of the cooking and serving utensils of a family. Glassware and china were known but they were too breakable and therefore expensive for common use. Pewter, too, while not as expensive as china, was nevertheless costly and, being soft, it was everlastingly getting bent out of shape, cracked, or even melted if left too near the fire. Our Colonial family sitting down to their venison stew ate with their pewter spoons with the help of pieces of coarse bread, and washed the meal down with mugs of cider. With the addition of a few more pieces of the same wares, as the family grew in number as well as in prosperity, this was about the whole assortment the ordinary early Colonial household would have had.

But in 1738 a couple of Irishmen from County Tyrone arrived in Berlin, Connecticut. They were to be responsible for a change in our cooking and eating practices and housewares so far-reaching and fundamental that we are still enjoying the by-products of their industry. They were Edgar and William Pattison, who arrived with their sister Anna, and they were skilled tinsmiths.

Pewterware and brass molds for pewter spoons. *New York Public Library.*

When one says that something is made of tin, like a tin can or a tin cup, one is talking about a piece of thin sheet iron or steel that has been dipped into a vat of melted tin. This causes a thin coat of pure tin to stick to the iron very tightly and for a long time, unless the piece is bent or pounded hard enough to force some of the tin coating off. The tin surface will not rust or corrode and will remain bright and shiny for years.

Tinware was virtually unknown anywhere in America at the time, but the Pattison boys seem to have convinced themselves that a great deal of it could be sold if it could be made here. So they sent an order to England for a few boxes of tin plate, and in the long months that had to intervene before it could arrive the Pattisons built a shop for themselves on what is now Hart Street in Berlin, Connecticut, just across the street from their home.

Making tinware at that time was, of course, entirely a hand operation. If you wanted to make a pie pan you first made one out of some very hard wood in the shape and size you wanted, but not hollowed out. You placed a sheet of tin over the inverted mold and pounded the tin down and around the mold snugly, then you turned the raw edge of the pan in all around and you had a finished pie pan far superior to any other kind available anywhere.

Unfortunately the records do not tell us just what utensil the Pattisons turned out first, but we can be sure it would be something that would be used every day in the average home of the period—quite probably a trencher; a lightweight, shiny dinner plate of bright tin would certainly be much better than a clumsy plate of wood or pewter.

A tin chandelier.

If we can assume dinner plates were the first pieces made, we can guess that mugs of some kind might be next and then platters and bowls of several sizes. Maybe a dishpan was next and surely washbasins must have come soon after. Having accumulated a little stock, Edward Pattison loaded two basketsful, tied them on a horse, and started calling on his neighbors. The shiny new ware made an impression at once; it was so much better than anything the neighbors had ever seen that in no time Edward was back in his shop to make more.

Soon he had sold every home in Berlin so he and his brother went to nearby New Britain where their reception was just as enthusiastic. By that time they had hired and trained some young fellows to carry on the production, while Edward and Edgar continued to go farther and farther afield for customers.

At about this time a Miss Tabitha Norton was married to a young man of the town and one of the guests at the reception, Emma Hart Willard, was so impressed with the table set in gleaming tinware that she wrote a few lines of doggerel that have come down to us.

> *Oh, what's that lordly dish so rare,*
> *That glitters forth in splendour's glare?*
> *Tell us, Miss Norton, is it silver?*
> *Is it from China or Brazil or . . . ?*
> *Then all together on they ran.*
> *Quoth the good dame, "Tis a tin pan,*
> *The first made in the colony,*
> *The maker, Pattison's jest by,*
> *From Ireland in the last ship O'er.*
> *You all can buy. He'll soon make more."*

All this was in the 1740's when, of course, no Patent Office existed, and even if one had it is doubtful that the Pattison brothers could have protected themselves from competition. In fact the hazy record of the time seems to indicate that they took the view that all America needed tinware and that they, the Pattison brothers, could not begin to make enough of it to supply everybody. It has often been said that an Irishman is apt to have more heart than brains but, be this as it may, a number of the young men the Pattisons had trained set up shops for themselves in Berlin and in other Connecticut towns. They carried on exactly as the Pattison boys had, making and selling and coming back again to the shop to repeat the process.

The industry continued to grow constantly up to the time of the Revolution when, of course, no tin plate could be brought in from England. Numerous attempts were being made in this period all over New England to set up plants to turn the bog-iron ore found in many places into sheet steel, but none of them met with any success until long after the Revolution.

But when the Revolution was over and we went on our road-building binge, the tin industry went into high gear. Now it was wagons for the peddlers and soon it was specially made wagons that could be drawn by two horses and could carry two tons of tinware. No

A tin peddler's wagon. *Old Museum Village of Smith's Clove, Monroe, N.Y.*

bells were needed on the horses of the tin peddler's wagon; his presence was always heralded by the jingle of pots and pans as the wagon rumbled along the new turnpikes and forded the streams. By the time the War of 1812 was over some semblance of system began to appear in the business. It was found that five men working in a tin plant could produce enough ware to keep twenty-five peddlers supplied, so no longer did the peddler become a production man in between selling seasons.

A northern, a southern, and a western route were mapped out, ranging from twelve hundred to as high as fifteen hundred miles long. Timothy Dwight, who was President of Yale University in the 1820's, wrote his *Travels in New England and New York* in 1823. He tells us that he frequently met tin peddlers far out on Cape Cod, on Lake Erie, in Ohio, in Michigan, and down in Kentucky and even up in Canada, and he speaks of other travelers having met them in St. Louis and farther south in New Orleans.

If a peddler was to travel a northern or western route he would start out from the plant in the late winter or very early spring in order to have as much summer weather as possible. If he was headed south where little snow could be counted on he would start out in the fall. Soon, however, another plan was devised. Six strategically located cities were selected—Richmond, New Bern, Charleston, Savannah, Albany, New York, and Montreal. Tinsmiths from the home plants were sent to each of these cities, carrying with them their tools and a supply of tin plate. Taking temporary space in each city they set up shop and produced throughout the winter. The peddler would have his seasonal plant in mind as he drove along his route, trying always to arrive there when his stock was about exhausted. He would turn in his cash, take on another load, and start the long road home. Many of them used to meet in New York where they would "do the town" for a few days and then head back to Connecticut.

By the 1830's the number of items made of tin had greatly increased. When all the necessities had been developed the factories gave their energies to the invention of new items, things that had never been made out of tin before. Regrettably, very few really old items of tin remain to us. They were not imperishable, of course. Some of the few to be seen are the candle molds and now and then you will see a delightfully shaped candle sconce in an antique store. Candlesticks, too, are not uncommon. By the 1850's plain bright tin became so common that much thought began to be given to decorating it, particularly those pieces that were to hang on the wall or to stand on a mantel. Varnishing was first tried. Since varnish first came from Japan, all tinware that was varnished was promptly called japannedware, just as fine porcelain came to be called china; it probably made it sound a little better than plain tinware and a little more money could be asked for it. Almost at once a host of decorators sprang up: not satisfied with merely varnishing the item, they added floral designs in bright colors done free hand with a brush. And I have seen one or two old pieces done in this manner by some nameless artist that are still a joy to look at. The process of japanning of course tended to protect the thin coating of tin over the iron and consequently japanned pieces are more apt to be found in the antique shops today. The Pattison family continued to operate their pioneer tin shop in Berlin until 1828 when Shubael, the sole surviving son, died.

JAPANNED
COFFEE POT

Catherine M. North, in her *History of Berlin, Connecticut,* written early in the twentieth century nearly a hundred years after the death of Shubael Pattison, has an interesting paragraph about the street where the factory was. "There is a springy feel under the feet as one walks through this street. A few years since, when Elmer E. Austin planted a row of apple trees along the side of the road by his premises, he found tin chips buried there the whole distance, and some of the trees died because the roots could not penetrate to the under soil."

A bit of verse, written by one Hugh Peters back in the days when the tin peddler dominated the highways, indicates what a familiar figure he must have been:

A YANKEE LYRIC

There is, in famous Yankee-land
A class of men ycleped tin-peddlers,
A shrewd, sarcastic band
Of busy meddlers;
They scour the country through and through,
Vending their wares, tin pots, tin pans,
Tin ovens, dippers, wash bowls, cans,
Tin whistles, kettles, or to boil or stew,
Tin cullenders, tin nutmeg graters,
Tin warming platters for your fish and 'taters
In short,
If you will look within
His cart,
And gaze upon the tin
Which glitters there,
So bright and fair,
There is no danger in defying
You to go off without buying.

One of these cunning, keen-eyed gentry
Stopped at a tavern in the country
Just before night,
And called for bitters for himself, of course,
And fodder for his horse:
This done, our worthy wight
Informed the landlord that his purse was low,

Quite empty, I assure you, sir, and so
I wish you'd take your pay
In something in my way.
Now Boniface supposed himself a wag—
And when he saw that he was sucked,
Was not dispirited, but plucked
Up courage and his trousers too
Quoth he t'himself, I am not apt to brag,
'Tis true,
But I can stick a feather in my cap
By making fun of this same Yankee chap.
"Well, my good friend,
That we may end
This troublesome affair,
I'll take my pay in ware,
Provided that you've got what suits
My inclination."
"No doubt of that," the peddler cried,
Sans hesitation:
"Well bring us in a pair of good tin boots"
"Tin boots," our Jonathan espied
His landlord's spindle shanks,
And giving his good Genius thanks
For the suggestion,
Ran out, returned, and then—"By goles
Yes, here's a pair of candle-moulds
They'll fit you without question."

Our Colonial ancestors, and many that lived after the Colonial period, were fond of brass. They loved brass things for their homes and for their personal adornment too. Of course they used a great deal of pewter and silver also, but these metals are more apt to be used for food-serving dishes, while brass was used largely for decorative purposes. If you have an old fire screen, a pair of andirons, or candlesticks of

ANTIQUES
MADE OF BRASS

BRASS WARMING PAN

WASHINGTON'S
INITIALS ON
BRASS BUTTON

old brass, treasure them; they will probably never decrease in value.

Brass is, of course, an alloy of copper and zinc, the proportions being variable depending on whether a reddish-colored brass is wanted or one on the yellow side. These variations also affect a change in its ductility: thus if a casting is to be made, a lighter colored alloy is used than if it is to be rolled into sheets.

Virtually no brass was ever produced in Colonial America until 1802. Abel Porter and his brother arrived in Waterbury, Connecticut, in that year and joined forces with the Grilley brothers, who had been making pewter buttons there since 1790. The new organization took the name of Abel Porter and Company (this is the parent company of the present day Scovill Manufacturing Co.).

They set up a plant in Waterbury to produce brass from its constituent metals, obtaining their copper from scrap. They made arrangements with peddlers to pick up old copper objects, thereby giving the peddler another item to be used in exchange. The zinc had to be imported from England. The newly made brass was cast in ingots and these were rolled into sheets in the rollers of a tiny iron mill in Litchfield.

The demand for brass was large and it increased each year. The clockmaking industry was already well started, the demand for brass kettles was well under way, and brass lamps became popular almost overnight when they could be bought at low prices. However, buttons may have accounted for more of the use of brass than any other single item. Our ancestors, both male and female, seem to have worn brass buttons on every possible item of clothing. Some of them were functional while others were purely ornamental. Until brass was made here they were imported from the mother country or they were punched and hammered out of old kettles. Again the peddler was the collector of old brass kettles which he either turned in to the button-maker, or as in the case of John Fitch, himself made into buttons which he then sold.

Button-collecting has become a fairly popular hobby

in recent years, and buttons made of brass are among the most prized. The number of designs produced seems almost incredible to us today.

Brass candlesticks, deservedly popular in our homes today, are of three types depending on how they were made. Those that were cast in one piece can be distinguished easily by marks of the sand on the under side of the base. A second type was turned on a lathe out of a bar of solid brass, while a third variety, developed in the early nineteenth century, was the spun brass piece. These are easy to distinguish as they were made out of rolled sheet brass. Usually the base was filled with lead to make them more stable. The turned and the cast varieties were almost certainly made in Europe while the type spun out of sheet brass were probably made here.

Another item of brass that was sold almost exclusively by the peddler of the nineteenth century was the cowbell. In these days, when a farmer's pasture is always securely enclosed with wire fencing, a bell attached to the cow is not usually necessary. But in the nineteenth century nearly every cow had to have a bell if she was to be located readily and driven in from the pasture. However the making of cowbells here never reached  the point that it did in Switzerland, where in certain dairy districts each family developed a cowbell with a distinctive sound that enabled the owner to distinguish his cows from those of his neighbors by the sound of the bell. The bells themselves were sometimes engraved or embossed with a distinguishing mark and since they are virtually indestructible they have become treasured family heirlooms.

Handbells were usually made of brass with sometimes a little tin added. They were used in country schools to call the children in from play and on the farms to let the men in the fields know that dinner was ready. Sleigh bells, which bring back memories of frosty nights under a clear moon with a bunch of youngsters huddled together in a sleigh, were also products of the early brass factories. I can find no record of their being peddled, but it is a safe guess that they were, because they were sold in a day when general stores were very few and very far between.

————◆————

STOVES

To many of us stoves were, in our childhood, so commonplace, so firmly associated with moments of comfort and cheer, that it is incredible to think that for centuries mankind got along without them, relying only on some kind of fireplace both for cooking food and for bodily warmth.

The Greeks and the Romans had fairly effective stoves for cooking but they seem to have been used only in the homes of the very wealthy—you can still see one of them in an excavated house in Pompeii. It was built of stone against a wall, with an iron grill on top of it and another at the bottom a foot or so from the stone floor. Fire could be built in the space behind this lower grill, and anything placed on the upper grill would sooner or later cook; but it must have been very smoky when dinner was being prepared. For the most part the Greeks and Romans of that early period depended on portable braziers, made of bronze, which were moved about as needed. But with the fall of Rome and the coming of the barbarians the stoves were discarded just as so many other things were, such as wheeled carriages and baths, luxuries known in Roman times but lost for many centuries after them.

Men continued to use fire, of course, but up to the early centuries of the Middle Ages the fire was built almost anywhere in the building and no special provision was made for the smoke to go out; it simply found its way out as best it could.

Then someone (we do not know just who or even where) thought of building the fire over against the wall and soon after that, apparently, someone found that if you put a hole in the roof of the building over where the fire was to be built more of the smoke found its way out and less of it saturated the air of the room. How many years elapsed before some genius thought of providing a pipe of some kind going from the fire up through the hole in the roof we shall probably never know. But if we ever do identify him he should be ranked among the truly great inventors of all time for he gave us the fireplace around which humans have gathered ever since. The chimney provided the fire with a draft that not only made the fire burn much better, but kept all of the smoke out of the room.

This could have been somewhere around the year 1000 A.D. The fireplace, as such, remained unchanged in any essential from that time on, so that when the early settlers began arriving in America in the 1600's they brought with them the kind of fireplaces they had known in Europe.

The fireplaces were highly inefficient, of course, since perhaps 90 per cent of the heat of the fire escaped up the chimney; if you stood near the fire facing it you could burn your skin while at the same time your back was actually cold. But the fire was pleasant to look at and warming to the spirit; it promoted conviviality and conversation as well as providing a means of cooking and warmth to those who sat near. And at night it also contributed light—frequently the only light in the room.

So all through our Colonial period every house had its fireplace. If it was in a pioneer cabin, which usually measured about ten feet wide by fifteen feet long, it would occupy one entire end and its chimney might first be built of thin saplings and lined with mud inside and out. This was only a temporary expedient, as the builder well knew it would not only leak very badly but would catch fire and burn before long. He replaced this temporary structure just as soon as he could with a permanent one of fieldstone or flat slabs of any stone he could get.

If the Colonial house was in one of the cities it might have several fireplaces; a big one in the main downstairs room of the house and much smaller ones in the other rooms. Fires were, remember, the only source of heat in the house. In the cities and larger towns the chimneys would be built of brick or stone from the first, as bricks were made in the colonies as early as the mid-1600's. A great many of our old Colonial homes still standing, particularly the larger ones, were actually built around a huge square chimney. The chimney itself gave a pleasant warmth to the inner walls of the house and a cozy little fireplace in each bedroom must have added greatly to the livability of those old homes. On a winter night those bedrooms would still be very cold, so that you would do well to warm your sheets with one of those fine old brass bed-warmers filled with hot coals. As I write this I have in mind just such a fine old house up in the area of Lyme, Connecticut; it proudly bears the date of 1746 and I think it will be there another couple of centuries.

Then along came Benjamin Franklin with his absolutely insatiable curiosity—he was never satisfied with anything; he was forever experimenting. He was not content to fly a kite like any other boy; he had to use wire instead of string and pull some lightning down out of the sky. Sitting in a chair one day he got to wondering what it would be like if he put rockers on the chair and soon we had the rocking chair. So we should not be surprised to hear that while he was sitting in front of his fireplace one cold winter's night he

The special feature of the Franklin stove is the flue which doubles back forms a sort of radiator.

suddenly jumped to his feet and said he was going to pull that fireplace out away from the wall so it could radiate heat from all sides instead of from just one side of it. In effect that is just what he did; he built a fireplace out of iron away from the wall with the chimney going back into the old fireplace flue—and the thing worked. It heated the room much faster, yet burned a lot less fuel, and thus the world had what has ever since been called the Franklin stove. It had the shape of a fireplace, but because it had four sides exposed to the air of the room a great deal more of the heat was given off into the room instead of going up the chimney.

I imagine Mr. Franklin had no idea what a revolution he was touching off with his new stove. For his idea caught the fancy of the public almost at once. For a while everyone that had any access to an iron foundry was designing a new iron stove. Overnight the shape of the stove lost its resemblance to the fireplace and became round or square or even oval. Then somebody thought of making the top of it flat and using that space for the teakettle—it was a lot easier than hanging it on the crane and burning and blackening your fingers in the doing—and we had the first of a long line of cookstoves. From that date on we had almost a repetition of the carriage-building binge of which I have spoken. Every town of any size whatever opened up one or two factories to make stoves. A whole new crop of peddlers took to the highways with huge wagons pulled by four horses; some of the wagons could carry as many as twenty-five stoves. The whole idea of a stove was absolutely new. Of course some people cried that it was radical, it was heathenish, it had no biblical sanction, it would poison the atmosphere—all the usual opposition that a really new idea met with at that time. The peddlers, however, were equal to the situation. When he got to a village a peddler talked the proprietor of a tavern or a general store into allowing him to set up a stove in his place of business, start a fire in it, and keep it going for several days; the peddler of course stood nearby to explain its working and to demonstrate its economy—the way it heated up the room hardly needed any demonstration.

Of course the tavern or the general store was the ideal place for such a demonstration, with preference being given to the general store when a choice was offered. Everyone in the whole wide community patronized the store so, as a modern salesman might say, you would get 100 per cent exposure there.

Wood was the fuel, of course, as coal was virtually unknown in the early 1800's. Harlan Hatcher, in his *The Western Reserve, the Story of New Connecticut in Ohio,* makes an interesting comment about this. "In 1828 the year after the canal began to operate across the Reserve, Henry Newberry shipped a load of coal down to Cleveland. He drove it around the town all day in a wagon trying without success to persuade the citizens to buy it for their stoves. The only person who would try it was Philo Scovill, manager of the Franklin House, who burned it in his barroom stove. Perhaps that was a favorable place to demonstrate its usefulness. At any rate the demand increased steadily after Scovill laid his fire with it."

Of course, by the middle of the nineteenth century the country store with its group of elderly citizens sitting around the potbellied stove talking politics and spitting on the stove became a legend.

The stove with all its advantages, however, did not win out over the fireplace overnight—far from it; it was a long struggle lasting from about the 1840's right up to about 1900, and even then it was the cookstove that held on a little longer than the parlor stove.

Most of us have had the experience of going through an old house and noting the boarded up fireplaces with perhaps an ugly looking sheet iron stove pipe sticking out over where the mantle used to be. The stove brought a lot of comfort to millions, but in recent years we have reappraised the old fireplace and brought it back for the beauty and the atmosphere it gives us.

8

Early American Clocks

For nearly a century of our national life the Yankee peddler absolutely dominated the clock business. Without the army of peddlers knocking on the door of every home in America the clockmaking industry would have remained the small thing it was in the eighteenth century, when only the very wealthy could afford the luxury of a timepiece. This can be said without detracting one bit from the credit due the ingenious Yankees who made the clocks that the peddlers sold, because, as we shall see, frequently they were the same people. Let us look for a moment or two at the clockmaking craft in the seventeenth and eighteenth centuries; I use the word "craft" because it certainly was not an industry at that time. In Boston, New York, and Philadelphia we had a number of excellent clockmakers who produced good clocks by the standard of the day.

Each clock was ordered many months in advance by a family of wealth. The clockmaker frequently had to start with some old brass kettles or scrap brass that he had bought from some peddler who had picked them up somewhere for that very purpose. These would have to be melted down and poured into molds of sand made just a tiny bit larger than the gear or pinion it would eventually be. Sometimes a little tin would be added to the copper and zinc: each master clockmaker would have his own secret mix. After these disks were cooled they would still be much too soft to stand the long years of wear they were designed for and so they had to be "planished." This must have been a monotonous process—they were placed on a smooth surface and tapped lightly with a hammer, not just for a moment or two but for many hours, sometimes several whole days. When they were judged hard enough, then another long drawn out process of filing and polishing began until each disk was the correct thickness and diameter. Next would come the filing of the teeth in the gears. (If you are lucky enough to have a clock that you suspect might have been made in Colonial days, look carefully in the area of the teeth to see if you can find scratched on them any guide marks that the clockmaker used as a guide in filing—these have never been faked to my knowledge.)

And so the weary work went on—actually several months of painstaking labor. The result would not keep time as accurately as a modern chronometer, of course, but they did very well—they were good enough in an era when hours and minutes were not nearly as important as we like to think they are now. When the works were finally done then they might be sent to a cabinetmaker who would build just the kind of case the customer wanted and the type of works would permit. If it ran by weights the works could be fitted into a frame that could be placed on a shelf (if the case allowed enough space for the weights to drop slowly down during the requisite number of hours), or the cabinetmaker could enclose the whole thing in a tall cabinet that would rest on the floor and you would have a "tall clock" or, as they came to be called, a "grandfather's clock." It is not difficult to see why the ownership of one of these wonderful pieces of work was strictly limited to homes of great wealth.

Then came the Revolution; the clockmaker with his great skill in working with metals went into gunsmithing; but by the late 1780's the clockmakers were back in their shops. In the interval a clockmaker in Kensington, New Hampshire, had worked out a device to

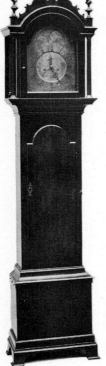

TALL CLOCK:
THOMAS HARLAND

help in the tedious job of cutting the teeth in each gear. Elisha Purington was his name and what he made was a lathelike machine in which he could mount his brass blanks and by means of a foot treadle revolve the blank an exact preset measure for the filing. This was probably the very first tiny step toward mass production in the clock-making business. Almost up to 1800 our clockmakers had been following the methods of the English and Dutch masters, but now we had reached the point where we were going to go out on our own. We have already noted the sudden birth of the carriage-making business and its phenomenal growth—the clock-making business was to do very much the same thing at the very same time in our history.

Simon Willard and nearly a dozen other members of his illustrious family lived in Grafton, Massachusetts (and nearby towns). And from the period of the Revolution on nearly to the Civil War they were turning out and peddling clocks, almost any one of which is a choice antique today. Simon developed several new styles, but he is noted particularly for the banjo clock. This seems to be exclusively the work of his hands, and those hands were so skillful that his design has never been improved upon. But he was more than just a dreaming artist—far more. He was also a production genius. Between 1802 and 1840 he made about four thousand fine clocks. His banjo clocks sold for about $35.00 as compared to many times that sum for the strictly hand-crafted jobs of the past. For the spirit was in the air those early days of the nineteenth century. A regiment of peddlers was fast becoming a division and soon after would become a real army and what is more they were now on wheels. Now they could carry fairly large bulky items and a huge market could be seen for any useful item if it could be produced at a moderate price. Just two things were needed if clocks were to be sold to every American home: a good clock at a low price and an adequate sales force.

Brass was scarce and expensive but wood was cheap —so why not design a clock to be made, as far as possi-

SIMON WILLARD

A WILLARD
BANJO CLOCK

Simon Willard was the most famous of the Willard Brothers. *New York Public Library*.

ble, of wood? The weights, the face, and the hands would have to be metal but all the rest could be of wood. Gideon Roberts lived in Bristol, Connecticut, but he had spent some time in the Wyoming Valley section of eastern Pennsylvania and it is supposed that he may have picked up the idea of wood from some of the German clockmakers there. At any rate, early in the 1790's he began making clocks with wooden works that sold for $20.00 (without a case); you could pay as much again for a case if you wanted a tall clock. It was a step in the right direction but only a step. It sounds strange to us now but in the little town of Bristol, where Roberts worked, no less than four other clockmakers were working on the same type of clock; but the man that the whole world was to hear of was in nearby Plymouth, Connecticut. His name was Eli Terry. Terry had learned clock-making over in Hartford from Daniel Burnap and in 1793 he made his first complete tall wooden clock. (It is interesting to know that Eli Terry's descendants still own that clock and that it is still running.) This clock was undoubtedly all handmade by the traditional method but it started

Terry thinking. As Eli Whitney is given credit for first applying mass production methods to guns, so Eli Terry is credited with applying the same ideas to the making of clocks. The basis of mass production is to make each part identical so that when you are assembling a gun, for example, you can pick up any one of a hundred hammers you have previously made, knowing that it will fit perfectly without any adjustment whatever. In 1793, after Terry had completed his first tall clock, he began making hang-up clocks, largely by the old hand methods, although he is supposed to have introduced water power to some extent at this time. He had one or two assistants and between them they would make four clocks (works and face only). When these were ready he would set his assistants to work on parts for another batch of clocks while he himself took to the road. He traveled horseback with a clock in each of four saddlebags. He tried to get $25.00 each for them, but it was not easy to find four families that were both able and willing to pay that much, particularly since each buyer would have to have a local cabinet-maker make a case for it.

Terry probably made only the scantiest kind of living for himself during the dozen or so years that he divided between making clocks and selling them; but these things were to be of enormous value to him later on. During that period he traveled much of western Pennsylvania and Kentucky, and he must have pulled the latch strings of a thousand homes. We can picture him sitting in a roadside tavern after a long, weary day of refusals and analyzing the reasons why people did not buy his clocks. The price was too high for one thing—if he could sell them at half the $25.00 he was asking a lot more people would buy them. And in the back country the time of day did not matter very much. The settlers worked from "kin to kaint," meaning from the time in the morning when the sun made it light enough to see by until it was so dark you could not see at night, and there was no advantage in knowing just what hour of day it was. Virtually all of the families that had left the settled seacoast areas to get a new start in the western wilderness came from homes that had no clocks; some of them may never have even seen a clock, and certainly had never had occasion to have one around long enough to learn what handy things they could be. And it was a fact that large numbers of people could not tell time even if they had had a clock. There was a further complication: no standard of time existed anywhere in the country. It might be two o'clock in one town and three o'clock or four o'clock in the next one. All time was "Sun time" and in the back country at least this was at best more or less of a guess. Certainly young Eli Terry must have grown discouraged at times and wished that he had been attracted to some other business. But we can be sure that Eli Terry the peddler exchanged experiences with many another peddler in that dozen or so years, learning from this interchange what an enormous selling power they collectively represented.

Back in Connecticut he sold his business to Herman Clark, one of his assistants and with the proceeds he set up a partnership arrangement with two other clockmakers, Silas Hoadley and Seth Thomas. This does not appear to have worked out too well, for we find that in three years (1810) Terry sold his interest to Hoadley and Thomas and set up a shop for himself in Plymouth Hollow nearby. During all this time Eli was doing a lot of hard thinking about how he could produce a clock that would be complete, case and all, ready to wind up and go, at a price much lower than any of the other handmade clocks. If he could do this he could line up hundreds of peddlers to sell them and he would really be in business. Terry, more than any other clockmaker, seems to have visualized what an enormous selling potential the peddlers of the country had if he could put the right item in their hands. And this is just what he did. He designed a shelf clock only about twenty-nine inches high, complete with all wooden works and case, known now to collectors as the pillar-and-scroll. It was beautiful, ran for thirty hours on one winding, and sold for $15.00 with a nice profit to the maker and to the peddler. Researchers differ on some of the figures—some saying that he turned out four thousand of them the first year while others claim it was nearer six thousand, but no matter. The clock was

PILLAR AND SCROLL CLOCK:
ELI TERRY

an astounding success from the first. Eli Terry lived till 1852 and had the satisfaction of seeing his two sons carry on his business.

Of course a success always produces a number of imitators. (Remember when Henry Ford brought out his Model T, which sold at such a low price that everybody suddenly wanted one of them?) A dozen or more clockmakers came out with similar clocks and some of them were very successful too, as, for example the bronze looking-glass clock by Chauncey Jerome. Soon the thirty-hour clock made way for the one that would run for eight days, and they went back to brass works. The reason for this was that brass production took a big jump and the price of brass an equally big drop.

Almost all of the clocks made at this period showed the canniness of the Yankee in many ways, particularly in the way each clock was marked—"Warranted if well used," which of course left the door wide open when someone complained that the clock wouldn't work.

Mr. Terry enjoyed success in his declining years; he could look out his factory window and see ten big two-horse wagons loaded down with his clocks and know that every timepiece would be sold and sold profitably.

With the drop in the price of brass and the development of better and better machinery, gear wheels and all the rest of the clocks' works began to be stamped out of sheets of smooth brass. Noble Jerome, younger brother of ex-peddler Chauncey Jerome, was particularly successful with the brass stamping method. And at the same time Chauncey introduced a brand new way of selling clocks. He loaded a ship with his clocks and sent it to England in the belief that with his price much lower than any in England he should be able to sell them. But as soon as the ship tied up in Liverpool and the English heard about his low prices, the customs officials seized the whole cargo as being unfair to their own clockmakers. They paid the price that Jerome had expected to get and so the venture was an easy triumph. Thinking that it might work again, Chauncey loaded another ship and sent it over and the same thing happened. A third shipload was sent over, but this time the British customs did not interfere and

SETH THOMAS CLOCK

so Jerome's agent had to sell them in the regular market—which he did without any trouble.

The role of the Yankee peddler in the clock business from around 1800 into the 1890's was tremendous. No figures are available on what percentage of the clocks sold in that period went through the peddler route as compared to established retail outlets, but there can be no doubt that the peddler had the lion's share. He deserved it—he actually *sold* clocks, day in and day out, frequently to the exclusion of every other item. And,

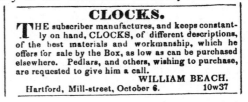

CLOCKS.

THE subscriber manufactures, and keeps constantly on hand, CLOCKS, of different descriptions, of the best materials and workmanship, which he offers for sale by the Box, as low as can be purchased elsewhere. Pedlars, and others, wishing to purchase, are requested to give him a call.
WILLIAM BEACH.
Hartford, Mill-street, October 6.   10w37

as we have seen, before he could sell a clock very often he had to sell the farmer on the idea of owning a clock at all, an idea that is hard for us to understand in a day when a watch is as necessary to a business or professional man as his lunch or dinner is.

When we read of the things the peddler had to take in lieu of cash for a clock we are not sure whether we should laugh or cry. Frequently it was a note payable on his next trip through that area which might be the following year, and if the farmer had moved and left no address, it was just too bad. The habit of buying clocks with notes became so common in the 1830's, and later, that men went into the business of collecting on such paper. But if neither note nor cash was available then the bargaining would really start. The peddler would usually have some advantage in a case of this sort because he would have to know—as the farmer probably would not know—the market for at least the more common commodities. This was long before the day of daily radio market reports on produce and livestock that make today's farmer the business man he is. At that time the peddler might know that the price of pork was away up in the nearby towns so he would offer to "accommodate" the farmer by taking one or two of his young pigs in exchange for a clock. Sides of salt pork in the early days were almost as negotiable as currency—everybody ate pork and consequently everybody either raised hogs or bought them from somebody that did. A bag of dried beans would buy a cheap clock from the peddler and the same bag of beans would be accepted at the inn for the peddler's dinner and bed.

Down South the mule was a common medium of exchange. The South had far more mules in the early days than the North had and so we had a period when the northern farmer was paying a high price for a team of good mules that the southern farmer could hardly give away in his area. With no communications whatever, the southern farmer could have no idea how valuable his mule team would be a hundred or so miles to the north. But the canny peddler would know, and there was another clock to grace the mantel of that family and make them feel righteous about having bought it for a very low price. It is easy to imagine peddlers heading up out of the South with a dozen or more mules tied on behind and maybe a dozen pigs in the wagon where but a short time before there were nothing but clocks from Connecticut.

To my knowledge the term "status symbol" is a very recent addition to the language—I speak only of the term, however, as the concept implied by it must be just about as old as the human race. During the entire seventeenth and eighteenth centuries only the rich could afford the luxury of a clock. A fine grandfather's clock solemnly ticking away the hours in the lower hall of a mansion was the expected thing, the usual accompaniment of a home of wealth and refinement, just as fine linen and silver were in the dining room. By the opening years of the nineteenth century this association of fine homes with clocks had existed for a couple of centuries, so that when the price of clocks began to fall to a level that put them in reach of nearly every home, the poor man would have been less than human if he did not react to the obvious advantage of acquiring one of them. It might not be a dignified and stately grandfather's clock, but it was a clock and it ticked, and you could refer to it casually when talking with friends. You would surely manage to give it a prominent place on the mantel, so that even the most casual visitor could

SHELF CLOCK BUILT
AFTER 1837

not fail to see it and be impressed with your substance and standing in the community. The peddler who was instrumental in giving you this prestige knew human nature, and while he never would make any direct references to what your neighbors would think of it he certainly would not fail to mention one or two prominent people that had just bought one from him. And so you parted with a couple of hams and maybe a flitch of bacon and hoped it would move you into more select circles and give your wife and children a glow of pride in your accomplishments.

Of course by no means all of the clocks carried by the peddler were good clocks; some of them would run hardly long enough to allow the peddler time to get back in his wagon and around the bend in the road before they stopped. But the vast majority of them were honestly made, and if properly treated would run for generations.

It was only natural that many of the clock peddlers became at least part-time clock tinkers. A call at a farm might elicit the information that they already had one of the things and it was no darn good—just didn't run. This situation could spell opportunity to the peddler. He might be able to fix it in a few minutes and charge them a small fee and be on his way; or, quickly seeing that nothing was seriously wrong with it, he could tell them he would exchange it for a new one for a small extra charge, thus acquiring a clock that to him was as good as new—plus the extra charge.

Of course after a couple of generations of clock-peddling the saturation point was approached, but we can be very sure this was anticipated by the clock-makers as well as the peddlers. The answer was: you need a second clock—maybe one for the kitchen or the bedroom.

After the Civil War some of the clockmakers began to make a few of the grandfather type again—not with the old Colonial craftsmanship; they had ordinary everyday works, but put into a tall case; they did look nice and quite a number of them were, and still are being, sold—but no longer by the smiling peddler at your door.

9

Where Things Came From

If you step into an antique shop today and look over the hundreds of items that can be found there, you will realize that nearly every genuine American antique in sight came to its original owner through the tireless industry of the Yankee peddler. In the earliest days his merchandise might have been commonplace or perishable, but once he had established his routes and learned to know the needs of customers who were growing more civilized and could afford more amenities in their homes, he carried those household articles which we now value as rare antiques: tinware, pewter, and china, old glass, Hitchcock chairs, brass candlesticks, spinning wheels, and looms, clocks, Kentucky rifles, even small items of jewelry.

Where did the peddler get all the items he carried? We know that up to the Revolution they came mostly from England; but with the growth of native manufacturing, nearly every town in New England began to develop its specialty, to make those goods which the pioneer settlers needed, then to improve on them, and to embellish them so as to delight the eye as well as to serve a useful purpose; and thus a tradition of fine craftsmanship and pleasing design came to flourish in the new states.

Tinware came from Berlin, Connecticut, as we have seen, but later, as the number of manufacturers increased, it was made in many other towns as well. The fabrication of tinware brought out a great deal of originality among the makers, because the only way a new manufacturer could get a share of the business was to come out with some item the others did not have. The housewife might need only one dishpan, one washbasin, and a limited number of plates and platters, but if a peddler came along with a candle sconce for the wall, or a covered pan to roast her coffee in, or maybe a Dutch oven to be used for baking or roasting food before the fire, he made a sale. He also sold light pails for carrying water from the spring or well and heavier ones for the milk, and five-gallon covered cans to cool it in in the springhouse too. And cannisters—from the tiny ones used for spices on up to the large ones for flour and salt. Each of these had a tightly fitting cover that slipped over the top and served well enough to keep the coffee and the tea, the sugar and the meal fairly fresh. Soon plain bright tin wasn't enough; it had to be decorated—things had to be varnished or painted some bright color and now and eventually a little freehand sketching was required on an item to be used in the house. Tinware is of course somewhat perishable and very few old pieces are to be found now; probably the most common ones still to be found in the antique stores are the candle mold and the wall sconce.

COMBS

Combs for ladies' hair have been made for untold centuries: whenever a tomb in ancient Egypt is discovered, at least one comb is found along with the mummy of some long forgotten queen. Sometimes they are of the type designed to be worn in the hair as an ornament, but more often they are of the working kind that the lady used to smooth out her long hair when she came from the bath.

Just as in old Egypt, combs were made of a variety of materials in the early days of this country. The earliest were probably made of hardwood, painfully whittled out with a knife, but these were superseded in 1759 at Leominster, Massachusetts, by combs made from horn. Enoch Noyes was the founder of this industry and some of his descendants are probably still in it. Enoch seems to have been a staunch old Loyalist and remained one all of his life. For some years he spent his winters in his little shop making up a stock of combs and selling them from house to house in the neighborhood. But soon Enoch began spending his whole time manufacturing and let other peddlers do the selling. He found that women could do the final polishing of the combs just as well as men could. They used very fine sand for the first polishing and then followed this with much rubbing by hand with a paste made from wood ashes and water. For nearly a generation Enoch Noyes had what amounted to a monopoly on the making of horn combs, but after the Revolution others came into the industry in Meriden, Connecticut, and also down in Philadelphia. The brass combs made in Meriden had an instant appeal to the southern Negro. Their shiny appearance took the eye of the colored people, and the peddlers, always on the lookout for a plus, contrived the story that brass combs tended to make kinky hair straight and to restore the natural color of grey hair. I understand that this old fairy tale is even yet somewhat alive in parts of the south.

BUTTONS

To some extent the button business was a side line to the making of combs, because for a time buttons were made of horn by the hornsmith. But early in the Colonial period buttons were being made from bone and pewter to be followed by ones of silver and brass. Today when the zipper has almost done away with buttons except where they are retained for their decorative value we have difficulty in grasping how very important buttons were in the early days. In the Middle Ages buttons were used to fasten clothing together; but instead of the button being slipped into a hole made for the purpose in the other piece of goods, a loop was sewn onto the material and the button was slipped into

it. By the seventeenth century in this country we had the buttonhole and an almost infinite variety of buttons to go with it. But we were not content to use buttons just to hold things together—we liked them so much that we wore them more or less all over our clothing. We still retain a few of them on our formal clothing though they have long since ceased to serve any practical purpose; for example, a man's jacket still has two or three useless buttons on each sleeve. They are a holdover from the days when the well-dressed man had several inches of lace hanging out of the sleeve of his coat that had to be buttoned up out of the way when he was called on to do some work in which the lace would interfere with his hands.

And on the back of a man's tail coat and his frock coat you may still find a couple of useless buttons. They are a vestige of the time when a gentleman would feel only half-dressed if he were to venture out of the house without his sword hanging by his side. These buttons must have been a little larger and stronger at that time, since they provided half the support for the sword.

Today's cadet uniform at West Point was the regular uniform of the army in the time of the Mexican War. It has buttons and spangles all over the front of it just as it did in the 1840's. A generation or more before this the army brought out a uniform that had huge more or less spherical bone buttons down the front of the tunic. Being made of bone they were white, and the soldiers wearing them came to be called "doughboys" because of the resemblance between the big whitish buttons and lumps of dough. The term doughboy, however, quickly died out when the uniform was changed, to be revived a century later in World War I.

Connecticut, with its army of peddlers penetrating to every nook and corner of the country, dominated the button industry at least up to the days of the Civil War. Half a dozen towns in the Naugatuck Valley from Waterbury down to the Sound turned them out by the thousand and still account for a good share of the volume.

Shoelaces would seem to be just about the most unromantic thing one can readily think of. But it was not always so. In the early days of the Colonies shoes were fastened with buckles. The buckles were made of brass, copper, pewter, or even silver, and their quality was something of a symbol of one's status in the community. The idea of opposing holes in the instep of a shoe through which a cord of some kind could be laced was not a new one, but the trouble lay in getting a suitable cord. However, Yankee ingenuity finally solved this problem just as it did hundreds of other mechanical problems. A man named Pratt, of Randolph, Massachusetts, to be known ever after by the name of "Shoestring" Pratt, reasoned: Why use up long leather straps by slitting them into strings? Rather use the long pieces for harness and the small scraps for shoestrings—simply cut them on a spiral from the outer edge of the piece into the center, straighten out the string by stretching, roll it roughly till it is round, put a point on it, and you have a first-class, full-length leather shoestring made from a scrap of leather less than three inches square.

Old "Shoestring" Pratt made a fortune out of his idea. He would spend a day or two a week driving his wagon around to the harness-makers' shops, the shoe-makers' shops—anywhere he could find things being made of leather, buy up all the scraps, and go back to his shop and go to work on them.

Pratt's Genuine Leather Shoestrings were strong and practical and were a real factor in doing away with the style of fancy metal buckles. He sold his output to the peddlers, and in the Middle West and on the farms of the South they were an instant success.

———◆———

For centuries some form of pocketknife has been considered by men and boys a virtual necessity. Chaucer describes one of his pilgrims as owning one. "A Sheffield thwytel bare he in his hose" ("thwytel" in Chaucerian English being pronounced "whittle"). The ancient whittle of that day was simply a piece of sharp steel with a handle made of wood or bone or staghorn. The blade did not fold back into the handle.

But during the eighteenth century the cutlery-makers of Sheffield developed a blade that could be folded back, and later it was further improved by the spring arrangement that we still use. With these changes it lost its ancient name of thwytel and became jackknife or Barlow knife.

Virtually all of the knives of the English-speaking world came from Sheffield, England, until in the 1830's D. N. Ropes of Saccarappa, Maine, opened up a tiny shop to make them here. Very soon he moved to Meriden, Connecticut, because, as we have noted, they made combs in Meriden and Mr. Ropes reasoned he could use the scraps of horn and bone, left over from making the combs, for his knife handles. These Yankees were very canny. For more than two generations Mr. Ropes and his descendants turned out pocket-knives by the thousands, selling them to the peddlers who in turn peddled them to every town and village in the country. Of course the noun whittle became the verb to whittle, a pastime that has served as a pleasant time-killer for men and boys for generations. Mr. Ropes's plant turned out a lot of penknives too—the penknife being a very small pocketknife kept on a desk where writing was done. The pens at that period were goose quills, and the points would wear down with use and had to be sharpened slightly at intervals; and so a small knife for the purpose was kept handy.

WOODENWARE

In the first half of the nineteenth century dishes for serving foods were frequently made of wood; wood was cheaper than pewter but not quite as cheap as tin. Cups (without handles) and bowls and plates (called trenchers) were the dishes that were usually made of wood. Many years ago I bought an ancient wooden chopping bowl at an auction in Connecticut. In spite of its having been covered with several coats of paint (imagine anyone putting paint on a wooden bowl!) you could tell by its oblong boat-shape and slight irreg-

172

ularities that it was a very real old-timer patiently dug out by long hours of handwork. I bought it for a song, but I spent a great many hours scraping and sanding, inside and out, to get rid of that awful paint. Eventually it was clean and smooth, a fine piece of hard maple. My reward was not entirely in owning such a rare old piece; I will always remember that as I scraped the inside of it every motion of the scraper on the bare wood brought to my nose the gentle breath of the spices and herbs that had been chopped in that bowl more than a century before. I had the feeling that I was being allowed to sense a bygone pleasure that had never been meant for me.

Ash, maple, beech, and birch were the woods commonly used by the old woodenware-makers. "Dish timber" was the term used as the woodworker grubbed about in the forest looking for just the pieces that he wanted. Very nearly all of the dishes made were round —that is, turned on a lathe. The lathe was slowly turned by hand by a helper while the operator applied the cutters, until in the latter half of the nineteenth century lathes operated by a foot treadle were introduced.

Timothy Gillette, in Henniker, New Hampshire, was one of the best-known of the craft. He and his son opened a shop in 1817. In addition to the usual bowls and plates they made cups and saucers and they also made hundreds of skimmers and butter molds. These last two items are still to be seen in antique shops. True

Small individual eating bowls and two drinking cups. *Mary Earle Gould's EARLY AMERICAN WOODENWARE, The Pond-Ekberg Co.*

to the tradition of the peddler, old Timothy and his son would work in the shop all winter, and as soon as the roads would permit they would go out on horseback, loaded with wooden dishes to be peddled in the countryside.

Up in Hingham, Massachusetts, several small woodenware shops opened up early in the nineteenth century. However they made cooperage rather than turned ware. This meant wash tubs, pails, dumb-bettys, keelers, piggins, and similar articles. These were peddled far and wide by the wagon peddlers.

Other workers in wood appeared too: the wheelwrights who made wheels for wagons and baby carriages, and even for spinning wheels. Most of the spinning wheels found in the shops today were made in Europe in the Low Countries. They required a quality of workmanship that was not very common here in the early days. When you have a chance to examine a fine old spinning wheel (and I mean take it apart) you may be surprised to find that it is not glued, or nailed, or even screwed together—it is *fitted* together. This means that the legs, for example, are gently tapered and fitted into holes in the body that are tapered exactly to fit. However, some spinning wheels were made here. The peddler who sold them would take them all apart for traveling and put one of them together when he sensed a sale coming up. The small wheels were used for flax while the larger ones were for wool. A spinning wheel has a long wooden rod, with a knob at the top, standing up at the left end; this is called the distaff. The spinner uses it to hold the bundle of flax, or whatever is being spun. She twists a little strand of this in her fingers as she feeds it into the arbor run by the wheel that gives it a real spin and makes a piece of thread out of it. In old Roman times, before the spinning wheel was invented, a woman would frequently walk about the house, or chat with friends, holding a distaff under her left arm and twisting the flax with her fingers. Centuries later the inventor of the spinning wheel simply moved the distaff onto a frame where foot power could be used to do most of the twisting and that is the spinning wheel that we know. Since the distaff has always been associated with women it is only natural that they came to be referred to as "the distaff side" of the family.

———◆———

While our pioneer ancestors were as fond of music as any other people, the conditions under which they lived did not allow much time for it. From sunup to sundown was the working day and after twelve hours or more of hard labor, food and sleep were a man's first requirement. Of course the peddler was continually trying to break down this resistance with whatever musical contrivance he might have on his wagon.

At first it was the lowly jew's-harp—he could carry a hundred of these in a small space and at 15 cents each he could make money. Probably next came the violin—never called by that name, but rather known as the fiddle. Factories were making cheap fiddles in the East shortly before 1800. They could be sold for under $10.00 each and while their tone could not have been of the best they did provide music that could make a crowd happy and keep it square dancing all night.

Eastern Pennsylvania, where thousands of Germans had settled, produced most of the instrument-makers. To many of these people music was almost as necessary as food. They made the jew's-harp but they called it the *rumpel* and harpsichords which they called *glorias* and melodeons which they called *bosorgels*. A pioneer family that owned an organ had nearly reached the height at which ambition could aim. It would make the home of that family the social center for miles around and the peddler selling organs was fully aware of the strength of his arguments. He would pick out the most prosperous-looking farm around, particularly one where there were growing children, arrange for a demonstration, set up the instrument in the parlor and put on a little concert. Then he would invite the whole family to join in and if this went well he would have them arrange a hymn-sing for the whole neighborhood. He might spend several days as their guest, but you can be fairly sure he sold at least one organ in that community.

MUSICAL INSTRUMENTS

PINS AND NEEDLES

NEEDLE "RUBBING"
OR STRAIGHTENING

It is hard to imagine anything more commonplace today than the straight pin. But in the sixteenth century things were different. Pins then were so expensive that they were presented as gifts to the ladies of a family on birthdays and other anniversaries. And when no pins were available it was quite correct to give instead a sum of money to be used to buy some pins when a supply of them did arrive. Of course this was called "pin money."

Pins are made of brass wire now, as they always have been, but up to about 1830 our brass industry in Connecticut had not been able to make a satisfactory article that could compare to those made in Birmingham, England. So we imported tons of the little things and huge quantities of them went into the trunks of the peddlers. At first the peddler sold them by the dozen and a little later they were packed one gross (twelve dozen) in a box. In about 1800 manufacturers began sticking them in a roll of paper in rows just about as we see them today. The safety pin appeared toward the middle of the nineteenth century and also went into the trunk of the peddler and through that route into the homes of America.

Needles are of course made of steel and are even more important than pins. It would be interesting to try working out what kind of civilization we would have if the needle had never been invented. Just suppose all of our clothing had to be fastened together either with pins or buttons. The first of the steel needles (formerly they were made of bronze) were made probably in old Nuremberg, Germany, and two centuries later they were being made in England, although the material for them still came from Germany. Until very late in our history all of our needles continued to be made in Birmingham.

IRON COOKING WARE

Next to the cast-iron pot that hung on the crane over every fireplace I suppose the oldest cooking utensil is the iron frying pan. Today the pot has ceased to be common, but the heavy iron skillet is still to be seen in almost every home. The oldest manufacturer of such things in this country tells me they did not open their business until Civil War days, and that all of the ironware made before that time was the work of very small foundries scattered all over the country. They must have been numerous, and some of them in New England, as bog iron was commonly to be found there. It was a poor grade ore which had to be refined a long time before it was fit for casting.

The main room of an established farmer's home in the Midwest in about 1840 would be a living room about twelve feet wide and perhaps twenty feet long. The fireplace was at one end of the room with a brick oven attached to it; this was of course the main room of the house and had been the first one built. With the passing years another two or even three rooms would have been added, including possibly another bedroom constituting a second or loft floor. The fireplace and its immediate vicinity were the center of all the activities of the family; there might be an Eli Terry or Seth Thomas clock on the mantelpiece and a pair of spun

An early fireplace. Note warming pan and Windsor chair. *Antiques.*

brass candlesticks; and in the fireplace would be a pair of cast iron andirons. Two cranes would be attached in the fireplace in such a way that each could be swung in over the fire or out; at least one iron pot would hang from one of the cranes. A new tin Dutch oven would be on the hearth and hanging on the wall would be two or more frying pans and an iron griddle for baking buckwheat cakes. Of course there would be a pair of iron tongs and an iron poker with a hook on it and at least one long iron fork to be used for toasting bread over the coals or broiling a small piece of meat. Sometimes the andirons would have hooks on the uprights, one over the other, to hold a long spit for roasting poultry or any large piece of meat. The family might even boast one or two trivets on which to set hot dishes. Usually a bellows hung by the chimney and this about completed the picture. Cast-iron firebacks were fairly common in the East since most of them were imported, but few if any of them ever found their way into the Middle West. Pots and frying pans and griddles made before 1860 are almost never identified on the bottom by the maker's name, but after that date you are apt to find either the name Wagner or Griswold. Another indication of age in a frying pan is the depth. By the 1860's they were being made more shallow, hardly three inches deep, while most of those made earlier in the century were apt to be four or more inches deep and to have legs. Since it had a handle, this type of pan was occasionally useful as a pot.

SPECTACLES

It will come as a surprise to a modern to learn that spectacles were sold up and down this land by peddlers for a full century or more. Exactly when or where lenses to aid eyesight were first used is not definitely known. Marco Polo records seeing them used in China in 1270 and Roger Bacon, another one of the many geniuses the thirteenth century produced, is credited with the invention of the telescope in the same century. His writings contain a significant statement. "How useful they must be for those who are old and have weak sight," which seems to mean spectacles.

One of our own geniuses, Benjamin Franklin, is credited with having invented bifocal lenses in the years before the Revolution. He and a few other men of the time are known to have used them.

No glasses seem to have been made in this country until the Civil War. Up to that time, and even now to some extent, they came from Germany. It seems, according to the optical manufacturers today, that one's eyes begin to fail to see things clearly close up and that to correct this fault nothing but straight magnification is needed. Lenses designed for this purpose only are conveniently divided into five magnifications—number one having the lowest magnification all the way up to number five, the strongest. This means that if near-sightedness is the only fault of your eyes you can get a lot of very practical help by simply trying a pair of spectacles of each strength until you find which one helps you the most.

That being true, it is easy to imagine some importer of German-made glasses demonstrating to a peddler how easy it would be to sell them to the older people he called on. And I can picture the peddler showing the housewife a piece of dress goods or some other article, watching carefully to see if she extended it at arm's length to get a better look at it—and then pulling out a pair of glasses and asking her to try it with them. All the housewife would have to do would be to try on all five strengths and she was all set. Of course the peddler could do nothing if his customer's trouble was not seeing clearly at a distance and we may hope that they had the good sense to say so when that question was brought up.

———◆———

POTTERY

Pottery as such is no doubt the oldest man-made dishware. Examples are found in the most ancient excavation sites that have been uncovered. The Greeks, the Romans, the Egyptians, and even the Babylonians knew how to make earthenware vessels. True, they were not comparable to the fine china of later years but nevertheless they were pottery.

Josiah Wedgwood, the well known potter of eighteenth century England, who had been shipping large quantities of his excellent ware over here, seems to have become genuinely alarmed in 1755 when he expressed great apprehension at the report that a pottery was to be opened in South Carolina. Up to the Revolution Wedgwood's and certain potteries in Holland seem to have had a corner on our business but when the war was over no less than a dozen small potteries in the East began operations. They turned out a crude stoneware that should be classified as crockery but it served a useful purpose in the homes of our people. By 1810 we were producing a heavy white ware that became known as "queensware" that is valued by collectors today. It was far ahead of the old crockery but still a long way from being china. By 1825 we were beginning to make some fairly true porcelain in Philadelphia and Jersey City and soon after this in Trenton, New Jersey.

BENNINGTON STONEWARE CROCK, c.1825

Things as highly breakable as china could not readily be carried on the wagon of a peddler, roads being what they were; yet the records indicate that a surprising number of peddlers managed somehow to carry some of it. A pottery manufacturer usually engaged peddlers for the exclusive sale of their goods—one in Ellicot, New York, in 1814 carried on for a generation or so and another in Bennington, Vermont, did business until about 1825. However their product was mostly rough red pottery. This should not be confused with another and much finer pottery that was produced a little later; this was not sold by peddlers; it was sold through stores in Albany and Boston.

CHINA FIGURINES

While they were not of Dresden china, American figurines should be considered as imitations of it, and some very pleasing imitations too. They were sold by the peddlers all over the Middle West in the 1850's and later. It seems to have been a specialty handled for the most part by peddlers who sold nothing else. They went from door to door with a tray of tiny figurines of ladies in old-world costumes, gaily colored tropical birds, dogs, and other animals. Many of these are to be found in the antique shops today, particularly in eastern Pennsylvania where they were made by the Germans of that area.

————◆————

BROOMS

In spite of the vacuum cleaner the lowly broom still occupies its ancient place in the household and probably will continue to do so. In medieval Europe it was a bundle of rushes tied around the end of a stick while in early America it was made by splitting a block of birch into many thin strips and tying them around a wooden handle. No really satisfactory broom appeared until we became acquainted with what has ever since been called "broom corn." Thomas Jefferson in Virginia did some experimenting with this as did Benjamin Franklin, but it remained for Levi Dickenson in Hadley, Massachusetts, to do a systematic job with it that is still paying off. Apparently, in 1798, Mr. Dickenson planted a few hills of this new corn in his garden. This produced enough for him to make twenty fine brooms, much better than had ever been known. The following year he put in half an acre and when that crop was harvested he found he could make two hundred brooms.

Mr. Dickenson promptly put a few of them under his arm and peddled them to his neighbors, who bought them gladly. The following year he planted a whole acre. This made twice as many brooms and to sell them he found all he had to do was to extend his route a little.

By that time some of his neighbors wanted to join in his project so they greatly increased their acreage and set up a shop in Levi Dickenson's barn. They cut their own handles, even arranged to spin their own twine, and they were in business. The brooms found favor everywhere and for a few years Mr. Dickenson had to limit the number he would sell to any one peddler in order to widen their use as much as possible. By 1810 Mr. Dickenson's plant and one or two local com-

SPLINTERED
BIRCH BROOM

petitors were together selling 70,000 brooms. However the time came when he had to meet some tough competition. Some farmers in the Midwest found that they could grow a broom corn that was superior to the Massachusetts product—it was longer and stronger and better in every way and gradually the manufacturing of brooms drifted out into the Midwest.

For a full century a couple of bundles of brooms waving like plumes on a circus horse decorated the back of every peddler's wagon; in fact they became the trademark of the peddler along with the jingling of tinware.

———◆———

PLATED
SILVER

Sterling silver was never carried by the peddlers, it was too expensive; but when so-called German silver came in (it actually contains no silver whatever) and then a white alloy called Britannia, much of the silver-substitute business went over to the peddler. Meriden and Wallingford, Connecticut, became centers of its production and still are.

———◆———

BASKETS

The use of baskets (and consequently basket-making) seems to be slowly passing out of modern living. In the America of our ancestors, however, they were of considerable importance. All of the grain crops were brought from the field to the barn in huge two-handled baskets: these same baskets served also for bringing in the fruit and vegetable crops; and then if not needed at once for other things they might be used to store some of the crops. Two smaller baskets of the same general shape except that one side was flattened were used, strapped across the back of a horse or mule, to take things to market and to carry home what was taken in exchange. If you lived on the shore you had fish baskets and clam baskets, and inland you needed cheese baskets and baskets designed for drying apples and peaches in the sun.

Allowing for changes that the white man can be depended upon to bring about, most of our basket-making came from the Indians. During the seventeenth and part of the eighteenth centuries local Indians made

Ox muzzle, clam basket, large funnel, examples of skillful weaving. *Mary Earle Gould's* EARLY AMERICAN WOODENWARE, *The Pond-Ekberg Co.*

baskets and traded them to the white settlers for things they could not make; but during all this time the whites were learning how to make baskets themselves; so that by the time of the Revolution nearly every rural housewife could weave a fair article if the heavier work of preparing the splint could be done by the men in the family. The ash and the white oak were the favorite woods for this. The tree was felled in the early spring when the sap had begun to flow freely, the bark was peeled off and the log allowed to lie in the sun for several weeks to weather. The entire surface of the log was then pounded with a wooden mallet. This had an effect which seems rather astonishing to us now: it caused the wood to separate in fairly thin layers and if these were cut in convenient widths they could be stripped off the entire length of the log. These were tied in bundles and sunk in a pond of water with stones to hold them down until they were to be used. Later hickory was used, particularly by the Shakers, a fact that can be used in dating any old basketware.

The same kind of splints were used in making chair bottoms, many of which are the treasured possession of collectors today.

———◆———

Among the small items that every peddler could be depended upon to have in his trunk or his wagon would be some straight razors. Until well into the nineteenth

RAZORS

century all of them were imported, some of them from Germany and the rest from Sheffield or Birmingham in England.

The razors sold in this country in the days of the Pilgrims were essentially the same in design as those made in 1900, for the design goes back before the Middle Ages. In fact I think it may be added to the list of things that were made so well centuries ago that no modern has been able to improve upon it, not counting the safety razor and the modern electric shaver which represent an entirely new concept.

But while the style of the straight razor remained unchanged over the centuries, the need for it fluctuated from period to period. In the early years of the present century, if you wanted to indicate you were talking about a very old man you would probably make some gesture suggesting a long beard, because in 1900 or thereabouts a man of seventy or more almost certainly would have a beard. Almost every man reaching maturity between about 1850 and the end of the century would have a more or less luxurious crop of whiskers whether he had just arrived at Ellis Island from some country in Europe or had been born and brought up here. In the last half of the nineteenth century almost the entire race of white men chose to hide behind a crop of hair protruding from the chin and hanging from the cheeks. The style of beard a man adopted seems to have been somewhat a matter of personal taste, although we can suppose that nature might place limits on some individuals.

None of them was any help to the razor-making business of course. You may find it interesting to recall the faces of our Presidents with reference to their facial foliage. The first fifteen seem to have been regular shavers, as their pictures show no sign of a whisker; but starting with Lincoln it was just the other way around. With the exception of Andrew Johnson every President between Lincoln and McKinley went in for one of the accepted modes of hirsute adornment. By the time McKinley entered the White House beards were on the way out; we find nothing more pretentious than a mustache after that and those too soon passed away.

———————◆———————

Today we take glass in all our windows for granted; what kind of window would it be without glass? But windows without glass were universal up to the early 1500's and the luxury of glass did not become common until the late 1700's in this country and then only in the coastal areas of the East. The making of dishes and ornamental pieces of glass is of course a very ancient art, developed in China and brought to perfection in the Venice of the Middle Ages; but window glass was something else. It required an entirely different technique.

By the middle 1600's the English glass factories had developed far enough so they could turn out small panes of window glass not much larger than a man's hand; they would be wavy and frequently a little cloudy but they would keep the weather out and allow one to look through the window. This was a tremendous advance over the oiled paper which had been used up to that time. These small panes were made by the crown method, which meant that a gob of melted glass was picked up on the end of an iron blowpipe and blown into a round ball-like shape by the workman. Then an iron rod called a "punty" was attached to the sphere of hot glass and the blowpipe broken off. Attached to the punty the glass was reheated and the punty spun rapidly between the hands of the artisan. This flattened the bubble of glass into a round sheet with a bulge in the middle which was the mark of the punty; you can still find it in the glass transoms over the doors of many old East Coast homes. This bulge in a piece of old window glass, the "bull's eye" as it is commonly called, is a reliable means of identifying the piece as having been made by the old Colonial method. However we cannot date a pane of glass very accurately by the bull's eye; we can only be sure it was made before 1840, and may have been made at least a century before that. The crown method was the only way used to make window

WINDOW
GLASS

185

glass here, or in Europe, until the cylinder method came in about the middle of the nineteenth century. This method made larger panes possible and eliminated the bull's eye.

Manufacturers attempted to set up factories to make crown-glass panes all over New England and in New Jersey from the late 1600's on, but without too much success. The process required a great deal of skill and experience, and England, with her customary watchfulness over her own industries, did her level best to keep her skilled glass-blowers in England. Consequently much the greater part of the crown glass still found in the East probably was imported.

Little or no window glass was peddled until about 1800 since it was obviously too heavy for a trunk peddler to carry in any quantity. But in the early 1800's, when the wagon peddler came in, it became a very large item in his stock. What a welcome sight a peddler with a load of window glass must have been to the settler. Until the first of these peddlers arrived, windows were boarded up in the winter and "glazed" with paper that had been made more or less translucent with bear's grease or goose grease in the summer.

FARM
IMPLEMENTS
AND ANIMALS

In the generation just before the Revolution our agriculture had advanced very little beyond the stage it had been in during the Middle Ages. Such things as fertilizers and crop rotation were virtually unknown and the only power available in the fields was human muscle with a little help from oxen; even draft horses were little known. Soil analysis and any specific knowledge of plant diseases were unheard of, and weather reports were non-existent.

Livestock was poorly bred, and hogs, while very numerous, were of the razorback variety and seldom reached a weight of even 125 pounds. In general they were allowed to run free and find their own food. Our poultry at this period had very little resemblance to our fine flocks of today. The Dominic was the common chicken and eventually came to be called the Plymouth

Rock. A few red-feathered birds were to be found and some white Wyandottes. To a large extent chickens too were allowed to run free to find their own food until chicken-wire fencing was developed in the middle of the nineteenth century. When they could be confined with this they were fed with scraps from the table. This led eventually to a very interesting and profitable discovery. Chickens allowed to find all their own food laid most of their eggs in the spring and a few in the

fall—the total per hen for the year would seldom run to more than sixty eggs. No individual can be credited with the discovery, but it was noticed that from time to time would come reports from all over the nation of chickens laying more eggs than the five or six dozen that were to be expected. Sometimes a hen would lay one hundred to one hundred twenty-five eggs in a year but the reason for this increase was not actually known until the present century. It was largely a matter of meat and fish scraps. If a hen had been fed table scraps that happened to contain unusually high amounts of meat and fish, egg production rose sharply. This diet, with the addition of vitamins, has now produced an average of well over two hundred eggs per hen and many flocks average more than two hundred and fifty.

The development of plowing, that most essential operation before any crop can be planted, is most interesting. Thomas Jefferson recognized the importance of the plow in the production of food and in spite of his preoccupation with government affairs he personally did some experimental work to improve the operation that won him a gold medal from France. Plowing, from the day when man first thought of deliberately putting seeds in the ground, was a difficult operation. Probably the first seeds that were planted were put in holes that were dug in the soil with the fingers and later this digging was done with a sharp stick. The next step was to scratch the soil with the stick in a line so that the seeds could be dropped and covered with an inch or so of soil, although grains were commonly planted by scattering with the hands far into the nineteenth century. The next development of plowing was to use the limb or root of a tree with a sharp point and have an ox pull it along, thus turning up the earth to a depth of two or three inches.

By the time our first colonists began arriving, a slightly better plow had been developed. It was made entirely of wood, but it quickly broke or wore out if its surface was not covered with tin. This plow did not turn the furrow over; that had to be done by a second man following the plowman and turning the furrow by hand. With this crude implement two men and four oxen could plow one acre, or a little more, in a full working day of backbreaking labor. (Today one man with a tractor can do this in less than one hour.)

In 1797 Charles Newbold invented an entirely new kind of plow. Its shape was so much better that one man with only one yoke of oxen could operate it. It was made of one piece of cast iron with no wood whatever to break or wear out. I would like to report that Mr. Newbold's plow was an immediate success but that would not be the truth. The farmers refused to have anything to do with it—the iron poisoned the soil, so they said, it made weeds grow. Iron, they argued, was foreign to the soil; why, anyone knows that nothing will grow in the soil of an iron mine. This ridiculous belief persisted in the minds of every farmer for about twenty years and Newbold died in poverty of a broken heart. However one farmer from New York State, Jethro Wood, had the courage actually to try a Newbold plow. He found it a great improvement over the old wooden implements. In 1819 he patented one rather like Newbold's except that it was made of cast iron in several parts, so that if a part broke it could be easily replaced. This was an immediate success; Wood was able to sell these plows as fast as his small shop could turn them out; but this plow had the same weakness that Whitney's cotton gin had—it could be easily imitated and was soon being made by every iron foundry in the country.

From about 1825 on the peddler with his big wagon became more and more a factor in the selling of farm implements. The general store handled the areas near the larger towns but more than five miles from such a town the peddler carried every new implement right out to the farmer and was prepared to demonstrate its use if necessary.

———◆———

The original source of water for the settler was of course a stream or nearby lake or a spring when one could be found. But the shallow well dug to a depth of fifteen to twenty feet was the normal water supply in the nineteenth century. A long pole near the well with a long sweep on it allowed a wooden bucket to be lowered into the cool depths and pulled up to serve

PUMPS

the needs of the family and the livestock. In the 1850's a chain pump was introduced to the farmer. It was nothing but a windlass with a chain running on its reel and several small buckets on the chain that emptied themselves into a spout as they reached the surface. The next advance was the drilled well which would bring water up from great depths. This was operated with a manual pump. In the early stages of its development such well equipment found its way to the farm via the familiar route of the peddler.

PART III

ITINERANT DOCTORS, PREACHERS, AND JUDGES

10

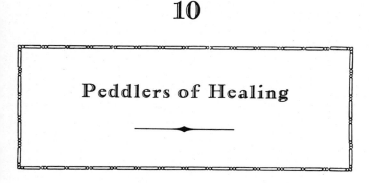

Peddlers of Healing

Ever since the biblical disobedience of Adam and Eve brought sickness and suffering into the world, the alleviation of pain has occupied the attention of a great many men. In the countless centuries that man has been subject to illness a vast amount of ingenuity has gone into remedies that for one reason or another were expected to bring about a cure. The list of panaceas is almost infinite in number and it has varied from age to age and from country to country.

In parts of Africa cults arose that promised to cure the wound made by a spear by merely touching the wound with the spear that caused it. Others believed that a wound could only be cured if you punished the weapon that caused it. If this seems absurd, remember the reverence and respect Europeans had just a few generations ago for the "king's touch."

Long before any written records were kept, however, man developed the idea that no matter what or where your illness might be you could cure it by "taking something for it." This will perhaps have to be scored as an advance over either of the African prescriptions but what a long, long row of concoctions it has led us to— and the end is not yet.

Harvey had discovered the circulation of the blood in 1628. This was genuine progress, but almost nothing of major importance in the whole field of medicine followed after that for two hundred years. We simply went on making elixirs and poultices and tinctures of every imaginable substance always in the hope that some of them might work. If you ever find yourself wishing you had lived in the good old days, or conversely if you want to be glad you live in the present century, consider the medical treatment given to General Washington during his last illness.

Tobias Lear was in charge of Washington's private affairs and lived in the Mount Vernon mansion with the family. He was present during the entire illness and wrote a detailed account of it two days after the General's death. This was included in *The Life of George Washington* by Jared Sparks in 1839. It was December 12, 1799. The General was living quietly in his home at Mount Vernon after many years in public service. At sixty-eight he was hale and hearty but on this particular day he had been riding about his estate for several hours. It was cold and wet and when he came back to the house in the late afternoon he complained of having caught a cold and a sore throat. This increased during the night but he went out the following day again and came back so hoarse he could not speak plainly and breathed only with difficulty. This time he stayed in bed and asked that Rawlins, one of his overseers, come in and *bleed* him while waiting for Dr. Craik to come. Rawlins bled him, all right, taking a full half-pint of good blood from his arm. This brought no relief, so, Mr. Lear goes on to say, they tried to force a mixture of molasses, vinegar, and butter down his throat—with no success. Then they wrapped his neck with a piece of flannel dipped in sal volatile and bathed his feet in warm water. Nothing seemed to help.

By this time Dr. Craik had arrived and Mrs. Washington immediately sent a servant to the next town to call Dr. Brown in for whatever help he might be. In the meantime Dr. Craik put a blister of cantharides on his throat and "took some more blood from him" (we are not told how much). Dr. Brown not having arrived they sent for Dr. Dick but what did they do while waiting for Dr. Dick? Once more they "took some blood from his arm." At this point I will quote directly from Mr. Lear's account. Referring to the last blood-letting he said, "No effect, however, was produced by it, and he remained in the same state, unable to swallow anything. Dr. Dick came about 3 o'clock, and Dr. Brown arrived soon after. Upon Dr. Dick's seeing the General, and consulting a few minutes with Dr. Craik, *he was bled again*. The blood came very slow, was thick, and did not produce any symptoms of fainting."

Of course, the grand old gentleman died soon after, probably with no more than an ounce or two of blood left in his body after having been bled no less than *four times* within a few hours.

I think today's doctors believe that Washington had a plain case of pneumonia: we can be thankful that the treatment of that disease has been greatly improved. Nothing seems to be known about any of the three doctors that attended Washington except that they came from nearby towns. They were probably average physicians for the time and place.

Edinburgh, London, and Paris had medical schools, at this time, that were trying to do a good job of teaching, and we too had one in Philadelphia. But the situation reminds one of Mark Twain's old story. Mark had just returned from his first trip to Paris and was eagerly trying to describe Paris to a friend. After a sentence or two he paused and asked, "Say! have you ever been in Paris?" When the friend replied, "No," Mark felt relieved and said, "Fine! then I can speak freely." That was the trouble with the medical schools —everybody could speak freely because nobody had been to them.

When our ancestors came over here before the mid-1600's their knowledge of anatomy was so deficient that they had no idea that the blood in our arteries was being constantly pumped through the body. And of infection of any kind, internal or external, they had not the slightest knowledge. When an arm or leg was broken or badly wounded in any way they knew, from experience, that it usually developed "a fever" in a few days that would soon spread to the rest of the body;

18th-century portable medicine cabinet. *New York Public Library.*

so before this could happen they simply cut off the limb and that was that.

As late as our Civil War a surgeon's first thought was amputation. And as for anesthesia, the deadening effects of ether and chloroform had been noted a little before this but would not come into general use for some time.

Since doctors who were actually graduates of medical schools were almost unknown, and doctors who had even "read medicine" and attained some competence in the profession were rare even in the cities, it was inevitable that a number of half-qualified men or amateurs should engage in practice. In late Colonial days and even into the nineteenth century, the practice of medicine was a sort of hobby for some men. Businessmen sometimes took it up as a side line. Governor Winthrop of Connecticut practiced it as a hobby in his

196

spare time, traveling about his own state, and even over the line into Rhode Island, treating any and every ailment that he came across, and it is said that he would even prescribe by mail for patients he had never even seen. Of course we may question whether or not his diagnosis would be any more accurate, or his prescription any more effective, even if he had had a chance to examine the patients.

A man could be a storekeeper all day and a practicing physician in the evening. Dr. Abram Staats of New York was a well-to-do fur-trader and a practicing physician at the same time and neither he nor anyone else saw any inconsistency in that. Dr. Jasper Gunn of New Haven was a surveyor, and when work in that line was slow he would mend kettles to make ends meet—in between sick calls. Another doctor, whose name has been lost, must have been extremely versatile for we read that while he preferred to follow the stage as an actor he also pulled teeth or bled sick people, and on the side sold medicines and ballads.

The formal, recognized practice of medicine evolved slowly, but as in every other profession in the early days the peddler had his part in it. Men who had some qualifications and could justly call themselves doctors took to the roads as itinerants; if doctors were scarce in the eastern cities it is easy to imagine how uncommon they would be in outlying settlements. Pioneers had to rely on some local sage with a knowledge of herbs or bone-setting in an emergency; in most cases of acute illness the patient died unless a traveling doctor was within call.

The peddler of drugs and essences was so closely allied to the medical profession that the line between them frequently fades from sight. A peddler of nostrums might end up being a "doctor," without having had any formal medical education; later the seller of patent medicines would appropriate the title.

During the latter part of our Colonial period and for the greater part of the nineteenth century a shelf of simple herb remedies was in every home. A housewife on a farm kept a little herb garden near her kitchen door in which she could raise sassafras, rhubarb, sweet basil, and maybe boneset, but those that she could not either raise or find growing wild in the fields she bought from the peddler, who tried to carry a big variety. Some of these simple herb remedies are still well thought of by modern doctors and we get some of them in a prescription now and then but probably not under the plain old-fashioned name it had in the past. But some of the mixtures given to the sick in those days make one wonder if the sickness itself might not be better. Listen to this one: A child gets diphtheria (called throat distemper at that time). This was expected to respond to a poultice made of pepper, mustard, and elm bark all pounded together into a paste and laid on the neck. This is not so bad but wait for the next—it was "snail water" which was made by pounding snails and earthworms together in a mortar. This mixture was dissolved in water and the child was expected to drink all of it that he could hold. Some variations on snail water called for the mixture to be boiled in ale, a collection of herbs added, and then several big beakers of it swallowed.

A list of the names of preparations sold by the peddlers of the day is funny if not terrifying, particularly when we note the troubles they were frequently *guaranteed* to cure. The word "cure" has long since dropped out of usage in medical circles as being entirely too risky.

In the *Connecticut Courant* of October 27, 1834, we read an advertisement:

> MOORE'S ESSENCE OF LIFE
> A safe and efficient remedy for whooping Cough
> Sold by appointment at the sign of the
> GOOD SAMARITAN

This is an unusual advertisement for that period—unusual in that it claimed to remedy only one ailment— and one had to make an appointment to buy some of the Essence.

Ward's Anodyne Pearls were a popular peddler's item. These were worn as a necklace by babies during teething. I cannot believe they would harm a youngster, but just how they were expected to help in the teething process is hard to see. And then there was Bezoar Stone. No record shows what this was but it was supposed to cure the bite of a snake; perhaps you were supposed to throw it at the snake before he bit you.

Turlington's Original Balsam was guaranteed to cure no less than fifty-one specific diseases. Then let us consider Dr. Spear's Liverwort Pills: the good doctor's claims for them covered about every known ailment and he had three thousand letters (so he said) from patients that had been cured by them. Dr. Spear also made a mixture that he sold under the name the "Balsam of Life" and it was a cure for consumption. Perhaps the high point of all this sort of thing was made by something called "Brandreth's Pills"—I do not believe this man even pretended to be a doctor but he was certainly eloquent in his advertising. Here is a small sample of it: "Remember in all cases of disease no matter whether it be a cold or a cough; whether it be asthma or consumption, whether it be rheumatism or pleurisy, whether it be typhus fever and ague, or bilious fever; cramp or whooping cough or measles; whether it be scarlet fever or small pox Brandreth's Pills will surely do more than all the medicines of the Drug Stores for your restoration to health." Since he spoke out against the drugstores and referred the reader to his local agent, we can assume that the pills were obtainable either directly from the agent or from the peddlers that the agent would sell to.

Even in the sordid business of selling fake remedies to people with real complaints there was a funny side. In the beginning a few peddlers went out with a trunk full of essences only, but before long they took on medicines too, and easily the most popular of all was "bitters." Under this name all manner of things could be sold. A bottle of (we hope) pure alcohol could have a dash of herbs in it, just enough to make it suggest a medicine and the farmer had in his hands a medicine that he could administer to himself just as frequently as, in his opinion, he needed it. Even if he was a deacon in the church he could claim he did not drink and who could disagree with him?

Of course through much of the eighteenth and some of the nineteenth century the farmer could make his own liquor (tax free) and he quickly found that some of his technical errors in distilling could be covered up in a fairly satisfactory manner by an ounce or two of one of the essences he could buy from a peddler. Essence of wintergreen might not be so bad and essence of peppermint would probably get by.

A product called "Tuscarora Rice" was unconditionally guaranteed to cure consumption. This "wonder drug" appeared in the middle of the eighteenth century and a great many packages were sold. We cannot even guess how many suffering people were taken in by this fake. The product was actually nothing but finely ground yellow corn. If the package had had on it a recipe for cornmeal mush or even corn whiskey it might have served some useful purpose but no, it was a cure for tuberculosis.

A Dr. John Tennent of Virginia was actually awarded one hundred pounds sterling for his "Seneca Rattlesnake Root" guaranteed to cure pleurisy. And just before the Revolution a Frenchman came over with a mysterious powder that he claimed would actually cure the bite of a snake, cancer, toothache, gout, and (believe it or not) it would even cure labor pains.

And then the case of "Perkins Metallic Tractors"— this would be funny, as the Irishman used to say, if it was not so serious. It seems that Mr. Perkins developed an idea that many of our bodily ills were due, in some manner, to electrical currents wandering around in the body without the sense of direction that they should have. So he developed a number of shiny iron rods that were to be repeatedly passed over the surface of the patient until, in some way that he never lived to explain, the wandering impulses would be straightened out, made to travel in the right direction, and one's troubles were over.

It happens that Mr. Perkins left us a fairly definite proof of his own complete faith in his metallic tractors.

Soon after he had them ready for the peddlers he contracted a case of yellow fever. Instead of calling in the best medical men available he treated himself with his own metallic tractors—and, sad to say, three days later he passed away.

In remote parts of our South there still may be found a few Quassia cups. These were sold in large numbers by the peddlers in the nineteenth century and may still be available. They were cups about the size you would use for coffee but without a handle. They were turned out of wood—usually some dark-colored tropical wood with a pronounced odor. You were told to fill the cup with pure water and drink it and then fill it again and drink it. If you did this three times a day before meals your kidney trouble would leave. The point is obvious: the water absorbed some of the odor and taste of the wood, which made it seem like medicine; and since most people never drink nearly as much water as they should, by this means the patients were induced to increase greatly their intake of water, and possibly some kinds of kidney trouble were relieved. At least no harm was done.

It is interesting to note that even before the Revolution, which was of course long before modern advertising was born, a number of itinerant doctors seemed to be aware of the fact that the public would be more apt to accept them if they could pass out some literature that they hoped would have an authoritative look about it. Thus we have *Doctor Jayne's Guide to Health*. I have never seen a copy of this but I am told that it contains nothing but praise for the good Doctor and his remedies. Why not? He wrote it.

Then there was *A New Guide to Health* by Dr. Samuel Thompson. Sam was an itinerant herb doctor who traveled about on horseback for many years, his saddle bags filled with remedies and copies of his booklet. This particular example of the peddler must have really been bad for we learn that he was declared a quack by the state of Massachusetts and forbidden to practice his "trade" there.

All this was *before* the day of patent medicines.

Early medicine show. *New York Public Library.*

Much has been written about the evils of patent medicines that we were to be both duped with and doped with in the late nineteenth century, but imagine what it must have been like when anyone could call himself a doctor and could dole out any amount of whatever mixture he chose to administer with no check whatever on what the mixture might contain. In the day of the patent medicine business the doctor was at least supposed to submit his formula to the Patent Office before he could get a patent on it.

Not all the doctors of that early period were fakers; without a doubt many of them actually believed in their own remedies. It is an old human weakness to remember the success and to forget all the failures. The fact that a remedy might actually be useless, or even downright harmful, does not rule out sincerity— one can be completely wrong about almost anything and yet have all the sincerity in the world.

Undoubtedly pure chance must explain the honest

faith that some of these early doctors had in their nostrums. A man complains of a severe cramp in his stomach; the doctor administers some kind of mixture to him; the cramp leaves the patient—he is well again. The doctor is convinced that his medicine was the reason that the cramp departed. And he goes on prescribing that mixture for all similar complaints. He does not know that the cramp was due to leave the patient from some natural cause anyway and that the medicine he gave the man had nothing whatever to do with the cure. The doctor will go on prescribing that medicine year after year, his own faith probably increasing as time goes on. Today the faith of our modern doctor in a new treatment is completely non-existent until its successful use can be shown in hundreds of cases under carefully controlled circumstances and by doctors of unquestioned standing.

While there were many obvious frauds among the early healers there were also men who were seriously trying to raise the standards of the medical profession. In the large cities, particularly Philadelphia, their work helped to keep the rascals out of medicine. But in the back country the quack who knew he was a quack carried on without serious opposition side by side with the practitioner who did not quite know what he was.

However, the back country developed a doctor who was different in several ways from his fellow practitioners anywhere else. He was short on formal education and training but long on honest effort. For some reason he usually wore clothes that were different— knee breeches when they had long since ceased to be worn by anyone else, a long flowing black cape, and always a high beaver hat. He was a real itinerant, and from the start always rode horseback. Weather seemed to make little difference to him: he rode about the countryside until he was called into the home of a settler. He carried a store of remedies in his bags along with some crude, rusty surgical instruments but he was prepared to tackle any type of illness from toothache to childbirth. If it was a fever he would sit by the bedside throughout the night, bathing the face of the patient. If it is hard to imagine the courage one of these country doctors had when he faced an operation, think of what faith the poor patient must have had.

———————◆———————

THE MIDWIFE

To the modern housewife and young mother of today the very word "midwife" may be unknown but not so many years ago the bearer of that title was an honored figure in every community in the land. Her function was to assist at the birth of a child. The prospective mother made a date with a midwife, who would appear at the appointed time, take complete charge of the patient, segregate her from the rest of the family, and be prepared to wait until something happened even if the birth was delayed for a month or more.

What seems to us really extraordinary is the reason for calling in a midwife rather than a doctor. To begin with, doctors had, on the whole, very little knowledge of anatomy, much less obstetrics, so there was nothing in particular to recommend them over a woman. But what seems to have been the main reason why a woman was always chosen was simply that she was a woman; childbirth was something that no male was ever supposed to witness. The midwife was called in primarily because of her sex rather than any particular skill she might have in practical obstetrics. Usually she was a middle-aged woman, frequently a widow.

This custom had come down to us through the ages but by the middle of the eighteenth century some of the titled women of France began calling in male doctors and from there the idea spread slowly over the rest of the civilized world. But the demise of midwifery was to be long delayed: in fact, there is reason to think that it may yet be alive in some of the more remote districts of the country.

When we analyze the situation at close range it seems that a woman who had actually officiated at at least a few cases of childbirth might have been more capable than one of the so-called doctors of the period who might be a carpenter or a stonemason during the balance of the week.

In the Phillips Street burying ground in Charleston,

South Carolina, is a simple headstone over the grave of Mrs. Elizabeth Phillips who "assisted at the birth of three thousand children." This does seem like a very large number but it may possibly be correct. In New London, Connecticut, Mrs. Lydia Robinson's claim of one thousand and two hundred without a loss is hardly nearer being believable.

The transition from midwife to male obstetrician started sometime in the mid-1700's, but it was to be many long years before these doctors could openly practice their obstetrics without allowing themselves to be known as "male midwives."

———◆———

CERTAIN CURE FOR TOOTHACHE—
CLOVE ANODYNE DROPS
Toothache dire will now give way;
Pain must end and cease decay—
Youth and age no more repine,
When they use Clove Anodyne.

THE DENTISTS TAKE TO THE HIGHWAYS

This jingle comes from a display advertisement in the *Connecticut Courant's* issue of January 11, 1845, published in Hartford. It serves to explain the status of dentistry in the middle of the nineteenth century and even into the early part of the twentieth. Dentistry as a separate profession had no existence before about 1830: any doctor would pull an aching tooth, and that was just about the extent of dentistry. When a young fellow reached the age of thirty or thirty-five he expected many of his teeth to be gone and, in another few years, none to be left. Decaying teeth were aching teeth; they were part of middle age, like going bald. The making of toothache remedies was a lucrative business for dozens of manufacturers; their products were sold by the peddlers and in the larger cities by the drugstores. Resident dentists were limited to the larger cities and they must have eked out a precarious existence since they had so little to offer a suffering patient that he could not get by his own medication. Before 1830 virtually all of the dentists were untrained itinerants, frequently tinkers, who, being handy men in general, could, if need be, pull a tooth at the home of a farmer. On good authority, I have been told that many of these tinkers prepared themselves in an astonishing way to pull out aching teeth. As they jogged along the road between farms, they developed extraordinary strength in the index finger and thumb of the right hand by constantly tugging away at a nail driven deeply into a block of wood.

At least one dentist, John Greenwood of Connecticut, must have had some foresight of the future of his profession for in the 1770's he actually made a set of artificial teeth for General Washington, and afterwards made dentures for a number of other statesmen of the period. According to stories that have come down to us through sources that are not guaranteed to be reliable, Washington wore them only on occasions when he was not expected to have to speak in public. We know, of course, that some of his portraits show him with teeth while others give the distinct impression that he was toothless at the time.

The world remembers Paul Revere for his famous ride and for the excellent silverware that he turned out in his shop; but if we are to believe his advertisements in the *Boston Gazette* in the 1780's he also did a lot of tinkering with teeth. His advertisements tell you that he has "fixed some hundreds of teeth" and that he will be glad to "wait on any Gentleman or Lady at their lodging." It seems to have been fairly common in the early days for gentlemen and ladies of means to have a tinker-dentist come to the house with his tools when their molars were misbehaving.

Nathaniel Hawthorne, in a trip through the back country, encountered some of our early dentists and has left us a description of one. This was written in 1838: "A young fellow twenty or thereabouts, pained with a toothache. A doctor, passing on horseback, with his black leather saddlebags behind him, a thin, frosty haired man. Being asked to operate, he looks at the tooth, lances the gum, and the fellow being content to be dealt with on the spot, he seats himself in a chair on the stoup with great heroism. The doctor produces a rusty pair of iron forceps, a man holds the patient's head . . . A turn of the doctor's hand, and the tooth is out. The patient gets up, half-amazed, pays the doctor ninepence, pockets the tooth, and the spectators are in glee and admiration."

Hawthorne also gives us a description of an itinerant dentist. He "has taken a room in the North Adams House and sticks up his advertising bills on the pillars of the piazza and all about the town. He is a tall, slim young man, dressed in a country-made coat of light blue (taken, as he tells me, in exchange for dental operations), black pantaloons, and clumsy, cowhide boots. . . . He is not only a dentist, which trade he follows temporarily, but a licensed preacher of the Baptist persuasion, and is now on his way to the west to seek a place of settlement in his spiritual vocation."

But better things were in store for the future; a dental college was opened in Baltimore in 1840, and the first dental society was organized in the same year. The following year state laws seeking to set up some standards of training and practice began to be enacted.

H. H. Hayden of Baltimore was the founder of both the new dental college and the dental society and it is

John Greenwood, dentist of 1806.
New York Public Library.

interesting to note that he had been a pupil of John Greenwood, the man who had made Washington's false teeth.

The itinerant doctor is gone now, replaced by the trained and qualified professional man, and by hospitals and clinics; and the seller of patent medicines is ensconced securely behind the counter of his retail store. Ghastly and ineffective as their remedies may have been, they probably brought some comfort into the lives of rural people, and if only through their inadequacy, paved the way for progress.

11

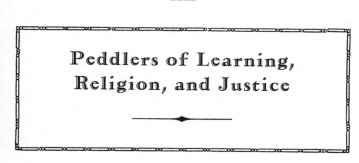

Peddlers of Learning, Religion, and Justice

If our ancestors depended on peddlers for goods which they could not make or grow themselves, they depended equally on itinerants for those intangibles without which their lives would have been incomplete. Just as a pioneer needed a traveling painter or craftsman to beautify his home, and a traveling doctor to cure his ills, he also needed a traveling book salesman to bring him the printed word. Since Bibles and religious tracts formed a large part of the reading matter of the pioneer, the man who supplied them was often a preacher; and the peddler of books or the itinerant printer was a man of some learning who would some-day settle down to become the editor of a country paper. The peddling of books and tracts, the spread of religion through itinerant preachers, and the progress of education and literacy are inextricably woven to-gether in our social history.

That the selling of printed matter of all kinds to the settlers from about the end of the eighteenth century on was a large item is surely some indication of their literacy, in spite of the fact that some of the reading matter sold to them was far from being first-rate litera-ture. What became known as a chapbook was one of the first types of printed matter to find its way into the peddler's pack. It was the forerunner of our comic

book and while it could make no claim to literary value
it must have served to keep the printed word familiar to
many an outlying pioneer. Next followed religious
matter of various kinds. The *Bay Psalm Book* by Weld
and Eliot, first printed in Cambridge in 1640 by
Stephen Day, actually went through seventy editions in
the course of a little over a century. It was too expensive and bulky for the earlier peddlers, but copies of it
were carried on the wagons when they came along in
about 1800. In 1752 Kneeland and Green, in Boston,
published a Bible that never seems to have been peddled
to any extent. Of course the *New England Primer* met
with great sales. It contained a catechism and other
things that were supposed to be taught to children including the alphabet and simple numbers. A total of
about six million copies of this book were sold. *A New
and Complete System of Arithmetic* by Nicholas Pike,
coming out just after the close of the Revolution, met
with sales to prospective schoolteachers just as did
Noah Webster's *American Spelling Book* which appeared in 1788. Then the *Farmer's Almanack*, first
published in 1792 by Robert Baily Thomas at Sterling,
Massachusetts, came out and is still being published
annually.

By the early 1800's, when wagons could be used and
particularly when they could be designed to handle
books, the sales rose steeply. Wagons were built with
high boxlike bodies that opened on three sides exposing
many feet of shelving. The customer could walk
around and look at the titles much as we can in today's
bookstore. With one of these wagons the peddler could
not only carry just about everything published, he
could departmentalize his stock—one side of the wagon
for the adults and the other side for the children and
young people. The selling of books produced its full
quota of queer characters. One of the outstanding ones
was Joseph A. Coe who came from Meriden, Connecticut. For a long period of years he bought Bibles
by the armful, tore the covers off them and handed a
page or two to everyone he could come in contact with.
He quickly acquired the name of "Bible Leaf Joe"
and is known to have traveled the country from the

Great Lakes as far south as New Orleans. What he expected to accomplish by this means is hard to tell and how he managed to make a living and keep his wagon supplied with Bibles for many years will always remain a mystery.

Peddlers also carried single-sheet publications known as broadsides. The earliest broadsides were really proclamations to be posted in public places and passed around a community for its enlightenment. These were, of course, not commonly sold by the peddler, but they got a lot of attention when they were pasted on the wall of the post office, the general store, or the stagecoach station and in the inn. At an early date enterprising printers began to profit by this. They would print up broadsides on almost any conceivable subject, sell a bundle of them to each peddler that came along, and both they and the peddler would make a quick profit. The confession of some criminal about to die was a surefire subject for a broadside, particularly if it was illustrated with a few skulls and coffins. And communications being what they were in the early days, we can suppose that the printer would not always feel that any restrictions were imposed upon him by the facts, or shall we say the absence of facts. Broadsides were yellow journalism in its earliest stages.

THE STORY OF PARSON WEEMS

Parson Weems, who was also a preacher, is the most famous of the book peddlers; ironically, he is best known for something that never actually happened— the old story about George Washington and the cherry tree.

His biographer says: "For thirty years there was no more familiar figure on the roads of the southern states than this book peddler and author who, provided gypsy-like with horse and wagon, traveled his long route year afer year, sleeping in wayside inns, farmhouses or forest, fiddling, writing, selling books, living in the open, and learning some new road lore, field lore, or wisdom of the road with each new day that passed."

Mason Locke Weems was born in Anne Arundel County, Maryland, in 1759. When he was only four-

teen he was sent abroad to study medicine at the University of Edinburgh. But his three years of medicine apparently made him change his mind for in 1772 he left the university and went to England where he became a minister. Once ordained he returned to America and served in the ministry in his native state for eight years. After this period he apparently became restless in his small community, for he became an itinerant preacher. He would preach on the green of any village, in a dance hall, in the public room of an inn, or anywhere he could find a few people to listen. In 1800 he added to his responsibilities by becoming a book peddler. He seems to have made some permanent arrangement for a supply of books with a bookstore in Virginia.

At some time he had learned to play a fiddle and so he was well prepared for almost any occasion that might come up. If, when he arrived in a village, a dance was scheduled he would offer to play for the dance or preach a sermon if that was more in order and of course at all times to sell from his stock of books. He is said to have sold three thousand copies of a fairly expensive Bible during one of his first years on the road. It was a subscription edition in five volumes, so we assume that he took orders for it and delivered them some months later when he had visited his headquarters in Virginia. He had another habit that the modern salesman would call a "gimmick." He would load his wagon with some book around which he could weave a story with an appropriate moral, and head for a town with a courthouse when he knew the court would be in session. Beside the door of the courthouse he would set up a display of his books and pass out circulars, even throw in a sermon—and he would also sell a lot of books. He had written a sermon against the use of liquor that he called *Drunkards Looking Glass*. We know it sold for 25 cents a copy and he frequently would wander into the bar of an inn and circulating among the customers give them a lecture and sell them a copy of his pamphlet. This eccentric old character carried on this activity for thirty years until he died in 1825.

His story about Washington and the cherry tree is now believed to be entirely fictional, a product of his active imagination. He undoubtedly had great admiration for Washington, and the anecdote had a sound moral tone.

A few of the book peddlers seem to have done well: for example John Dunton of Massachusetts and Jim Gray from the same place; each of them left their families well provided for. However, most book peddlers, sooner or later, did as the peddlers in other lines did: found a likely spot and settled down to respectability as a local merchant with a permanent location.

Some book peddlers carried nothing but religious tracts; they were called colporteurs and were a special kind of peddler, in that they were trained and sent out by a central organization. To meet the needs of remote communities for religious literature, The American Tract Society was organized in 1841 and Russell B. Cook directed its efforts. Between the founding date and 1856 he had trained and sent out into the highways and byways of the country an army of salesmen. These men worked all year but during the summer vacations another army of students supplemented them. His regular all-year force amounted to about 550 men; they traveled by every means available—by horse, on foot, on trains and boats and wagons—selling Bibles, tracts, and religious literature in general. Some of the titles may be familiar: *Examine Your Hopes for Eternity, The Lost Soul, Nelson's Anxious Inquirer, Pike's Persuasives to Early Piety.*

These people must have been good peddlers, for, if we can believe the records of the Society, in 1859 a total of three million families had been visited and the monumental total of eight million pieces of literature distributed.

THE ITINERANT PREACHER

Before we can understand these peddlers of the Word, we have to examine the political status of religion in early America. With the exception of the Maryland colony (and even there it did not last very long) religious liberty did not exist in this country until modern times. Early textbooks to the contrary notwithstanding, the first settlers in Massachusetts did not come here in search of religious liberty; quite the opposite—what they wanted might better be called "religious license" or the freedom to follow their own convictions and at the same time prevent those who disagreed with them from following theirs. This is seen in their expulsion from Boston of Roger Williams with his Baptist leanings, and the banishment and, in at least four instances, actual hanging of Quakers. In the South the only difference was in the viewpoint; to the southerners Puritanism was an infection that must not be allowed to develop in their colonies. The Quakers in Pennsylvania were more tolerant but even they imposed a tax of twenty shillings on every Irishman—"being Papist to prevent the growth of popery by the importation of too great a number of them into the province." The Quakers also viewed with alarm the emigration of Presbyterian Scotch-Irish lest they take control of affairs. In Virginia the Presbyterians were allowed to stay only if they settled a strip of territory that would act as a buffer state between the Established Church and the Indian country. Today we pride ourselves on our complete separation of Church and State, but in the colonies the prevailing situation was the exact opposite. For the state to make laws carefully restricting the practice of religion seemed to the colonists at that time its natural right.

When the Constitution was in its formative stages in Philadelphia some real progress toward toleration was evident. Virginia and Rhode Island now required no religious qualification either for voting or for the holding of office. Six colonies, however, insisted on some form of Protestantism, while two others were satisfied if you were a Christian; four demanded a belief in the divine inspiration of the Bible and two were satisfied if you believed in heaven and hell. In five of the colonies even at this late date the prevailing church was a state establishment. These were Massachusetts, South Carolina, Connecticut, Maryland, and New Hampshire.

An itinerant preacher on stage.
New York Public Library.

But with the coming of peace after the Revolution and the general acceptance of the new Constitution and its precious Bill of Rights which included the precept that "Congress shall make no law respecting an establishment of religion, or prohibiting the free exercise thereof . . ." a slow but sure abatement of animosities began. The Massachusetts Congregationalist had fought the Revolution alongside of a high-church Episcopalian from Virginia and the Dutch Reformed New Yorker for the same reason had found that his Irish tentmate (Roman Catholic) was just as patriotic as he was; we were on the way to better understanding.

With the close of the war, and the release of energies that could then be turned into productive channels, the tide of settlers poured out of the East into the western wilderness. Through the Mohawk Valley went an enormous stream of home-seekers and through the mountain passes of Pennsylvania wave upon wave of families went into Ohio, Kentucky, Indiana, and Illinois. From Virginia and the Carolinas went still more into the broad valleys of Tennessee and Missouri. They carried their religion wth them, we may be sure, but in the wilderness they found themselves faced daily with the immediate and ever-present problem of surviving the Indians as well as starvation. This preoccupation with survival caused a diminution of fervor that was, however, temporary in character; for by the end of the eighteenth century a torrent of itinerant preachers followed the trails of the settlers and fanned out into every settlement. From Philadelphia, in 1784, the Methodists sent a hundred and four traveling preachers out onto the highways of the country, and by about 1800 they had increased this number to over three hundred. Theologically speaking vast numbers of them were ill-prepared; but what they lacked in formal training they tried to make up for in enthusiasm; in the willingness to sacrifice personal comfort, many of them approached the discipline of the monks of the Middle Ages. The early Methodists did not marry in the belief that it would dilute their energies in preaching, Bishops Asbury and McKendree being prime examples of this sacrifice.

The practical problems of living faced every

preacher of the Word, and many of the men solved them by dividing their time between productive work and preaching. This might mean that a preacher rode from one settlement to another and preached when he arrived in the evening. Woolman the Quaker was a Quaker every day in the week but on six of those seven days he worked as a tailor. However, he finally reached a point at which, according to his writings, he "perceived that merchandise be attended by much cumber"; he gave up the making of clothing and gave his whole time to preaching. Devereau Jarrett, who was an itinerant preacher all over Alabama for many years, worked as a carpenter weekdays. The well-known Samuel Seabury, the first Episcopalian bishop in this country, practiced medicine along with his work as a missionary. In North Carolina David Caldwell was a doctor, a school teacher, and a carpenter, and, in between, a preacher. He traveled that state for many years, always announcing himself as a preacher first but willing to serve in one of the other capacities if it seemed more suitable.

Bishop Seabury was granted a salary of $64.00 a year by the Episcopal Conference with a little more to be added in case he had a wife and children; but please note—the Conference did not agree to pay even this

The Rt. Rev. William White, Bishop of Pennsylvania *(Left)* and the Rt. Rev. Samuel Seabury, Bishop of Connecticut *(Right)*. *New York Public Library.*

miserable amount; they agreed to allow him to collect that amount from his audiences if he was able to do so. Later they are said to have given more thought to this and raised the allowance to the princely sum of $80.00 with $14.00 for each child. He still had to do his own collecting, however. This was often difficult, since a vast number of people felt that they were doing their full duty when they merely sat and listened to a sermon.

Education and refinement were not the mark of the itinerant peddler of the Word any more than of the other types of peddler. Before the temperance movement had made any real progress many of them sustained their efforts on long trips by close application to a pocket flask and to a mouthful of "eatin' tobacco"; one in particular was from Indiana and it is said that he regularly interrupted every sermon on a two-minute schedule to spit on the floor of the pulpit, so that at the end of the service the floor around him was as filthy as a stable.

The Presbyterian, Congregational, and Episcopalian itinerants were apt to have had some schooling, but this was not always true of the Methodists, according to Peter Cartright who was one of them.

[We] had little or no education; no books and no time to read or study them if we could have had them. We had no colleges nor even a respectable common school within a hundred miles of us. . . . It is true not many of us could conjugate a verb, or parse a sentence, and murdered the King's english almost every lick. . . . A methodist in those days, when he felt that God had called him to preach, instead of hunting up a college or a Biblical institute, hunted up a hardy poney, or a horse, and some traveling apparatus, and with his library always at hand, namely Bible, Hymn Book and Discipline, he started, and with a text that never wore out or grew stale he cried 'Behold the Lamb of God, that taketh away the sin of the world.' In this way he went through stormes of wind, hail, snow and rain; climbed hills and mountains, traversed valleys, plunged through swamps, swam swollen streams, lay out at night, wet weary and hungry, held his horse by the bridle all night, or tied him to a limb, slept with his saddle, or saddle bags for a pillow, and his old big coat or blanket, if he had any, for covering. Often he slept in dirty cabins, on earthen floors, before the fire: ate roasting ears for bread, drank buttermilk for coffee, or sage tea for imperial; took with a hearty zest, deer or bear meat, or wild turkey for breakfast, dinner and supper, if he could get it. His text was always ready: 'Behold the Lamb of God, etc.' This was old fashioned Methodist fare and fortune.

In the rare communities where there was a church the circuit rider's work was easier, but church buildings were scarce in the early days. The usual thing for a preacher when he arrived in a town was to go from house to house, knock on the door and ask, "Sister, shall I pray with you?" If he was asked to come in he gathered the family together, led them in prayer, sang a few hymns, and was usually asked to stay for supper and overnight.

Bishop Seabury is said to have traveled no less than 6,000 miles through the back country over the period of eleven years that he served, while Bishop Asbury of the Methodists is supposed to have traveled 270,000 miles during his long term of service. He ordained 4,000 ministers and presided over 220 conferences. Jesse Lee, who operated in New England, is said to have made 6,000 converts and ordained 50 preachers in an area that had always been dominated by the Congregationalists.

However Peter Cartright is credited with being the most effective peddler of the Word. He served over a period of 50 years, during which he preached 14,000 sermons, baptized 12,000 people, and conducted some 500 funerals.

———————◆———————

THE CAMP MEETING

The camp meeting is a peculiarly American custom and Peter Cartright is commonly credited with its development. He was so successful with it, however, that the Baptists and the Presbyterians soon copied his methods.

The back country of America in the early 1800's was settled by an almost infinite variety of people; from the honest, ambitious settler who wished only to make a home and a decent living for his family to the rascal without a trace of decency in his makeup. Drinking and gambling were practiced everywhere, murder was an accepted fact of life, and sexual irregularities enjoyed a toleration that is a trifle hard to understand now. Temperance, which later led to prohibition, was a movement that started around the middle of the nineteenth century; in the opening years of the century, excessive drinking was so common that nothing was thought of it. At such events as weddings, funerals, and even ordinations truly prodigious amounts of home-made liquor were consumed. When the Reverend Edwin Jackson was ordained at Woburn the itemized list of expenses on that occasion show that the congregation drank six and a half barrels of cider, twenty-five gallons of wine, two gallons of brandy, and four gallons of rum. On the occasion of the building of a new meeting house sixty men worked on it for one week and during that week they consumed sixty-nine gallons of rum besides several barrels of beer and cider. Generally speaking the people were a rough and ready lot; they had little education and they worked at back-breaking labor from sunrise to sunset; they had no amusements and lived so far apart that their social intercourse was almost non-existent.

It was into this kind of society that the camp meeting came with all that it offered in excitement. The first of record was in the winter of 1799–1800. The Methodists began it but the Presbyterians joined forces with them. According to witnesses fully three thousand people fainted from religious ecstasy and had to be laid out

Peter Cartwright is credited with the development of camp meeting.

like cordwood till they recovered. Let me quote Cartright again, since he was probably in a better position to know about these things than any other man ever was.

No matter whether they were saints or sinners, they would be taken under a warm song or sermon, and seized with a convulsive jerking all over, which they could not, by any possibility, avoid, and the more they resisted the more they jerked. If they would not strive against it, and pray in good earnest, the jerking would usually abate. I have seen more than five hundred persons jerking at one time.

Most usually persons taken with the jerks, to obtain relief, as they said, would rize up and dance. Some would run, but could not get away. Some would resist; on such the jerks were generally very severe.

Camp meetings were commonly held once a year and then only in the farmers' slack season. A likely place would be selected and some temporary buildings thrown up, and in would come the crowds from fifty to one hundred miles away. They came on foot, on horseback, and in wagons and brought food enough to last for several days. One such meeting is said to have had an attendance of 20,000 people, and over 1,100 wagons were counted. The women slept in the wagons and the men slept under them. A weird sight it must have made. A thousand camp fires burning in the forest and as many as a dozen ministers haranguing great knots of people as far as the eye could reach. When one minister became exhausted another quickly stepped into his place and the sermon continued.

The Baptist war cry was "Water! Water! Follow your Lord down into the water." As Richardson Wright says, "So insistent were they on immersion that people began to believe Heaven was on an island and you had to swim to it." The Methodists proclaimed their superiority in a little rhyme that went:

I'll tell you who the Lord likes best—
It is the shoutin' Methodist.

The language of many of these ministers may have been biblical but it certainly was not charitable. Cartright admits calling a competing church a "trash trap" and he goes on to say that if one minister could not convert his opponents he launched forth on a description of the sort of hell to which they and their friends were bound to go.

Here are the gentle epithets applied by one of these traveling ministers to one of another theological persuasion: he was a "hireling, a caterpillar, a letter-learned Pharisee, a hypocrite, a varlet, a seed of the serpent, a foolish builder whom the Devil drives into the ministry, a dead dog that cannot bark, a blind man, men possessed of the Devil, a rebel and enemy of God." Not a real swear word in the lot but nevertheless some very fancy name-calling. And this is not entirely a lost art; twentieth-century revivalists still use it on some public occasions.

These camp meetings were beyond question the major social event of the year throughout great areas of our country in the nineteenth century. Friends met to renew old acquaintance, new friendships were made, romance came to many that might have been passed by, news was exchanged, and between sermons the political situation in the state and in the nation could be thrashed out; all this is conceded, but whether or not the good accomplished outweighs the harm is now difficult to say.

SOME SECULAR WORK OF TRAVELING CHURCHMEN

On numerous occasions throughout our history individual ministers have been called upon to serve their state or the nation on diplomatic missions of considerable importance and the results have been uniformly good. William Savery, for example, was of lasting service to the government in settling the trouble between the Ohio Indians and the whites in the early 1800's. Peter Gibault, a Jesuit, was so influential in holding the Illinois country loyal to us in 1778 that the Legislature of Virginia thanked him publicly for it and Peter de Smet, another Jesuit, is said to have had a magical effect in keeping the Indians of the far West friendly to us. Richardson Wright says of him,

"A great traveler Fr. de Smet, he covered in his career 180,000 miles by boat, canoe, dog sled, wagon, horse and foot. It is said of him that he was more powerful than an army with banners. In fact, he was a solitary soldier with a banner, for when he went to pacify Sitting Bull he approached the old chieftain through ranks of painted warriors holding a banner of the Virgin in his hand. That one mission brought 50,000 Indians into allegiance with the government."

There is also the story of Manasseh Cutler, the Congregational minister in Ipswich, Massachusetts. When the whole area of what is now southeastern Ohio was thrown open to settlement in 1787, Mr. Cutler inspired and organized a band of his congregation under the direct leadership of General Rufus Putnam to go out to the Ohio country and make a permanent settlement. He gave preference to veterans of the Revolution and they settled a spot on the Ohio River that we now know as Marietta. The good parson joined them personally about one year later. This was the first permanent white settlement in Ohio.

And the story of Demetrius Augustine Gallitzin is well worth retelling. Gallitzin, Pennsylvania, bears his name today. He was a Russian of noble family and his parents were atheist followers of Voltaire. Coming for a visit to this country he met Bishop Carroll of Baltimore, and in the course of a few years the young man left the Voltairean jungle and became a Roman Catholic priest.

After assigning Gallitzin for a few years to service in small, local parishes the Bishop sent him into the wilderness of western Pennsylvania to what is now Cambria County. The area was about as wild and primitive, in 1798, as any place could be, but the good Father bought himself a horse and a camping outfit and took to the trails to get acquainted with his "congregation." He never once used his noble title in the forty years of service he gave to the county, but he did make use of the $150,000 fortune that went with it. He bought huge tracts of land and sold or gave it to his followers for the proverbial song.

ITINERANT JUSTICE

It is natural that our judicial system should have derived many of its characteristics from that of England. There, from the time of the Norman conquest, the king's justice was dispensed in a series of assize courts set up at convenient points around the country. Judges traveled regularly on this circuit by horseback in early days, and in the eighteenth century by stage-coach.

In 1798 our new Constitution provided for a judiciary branch of the government, and Congress duly set it up: in addition to the Supreme Court, with its chief justice and associate justices, there were thirteen district courts and three circuits. The three circuits were in the East, the Middle West, and the South, with a court for each consisting of two judges of the Supreme Court and a judge from the district where the particular court was held. On April 4, 1790, the First Circuit Court in the Eastern division was held with Chief Justice Jay, Judge Cushing, and District Judge Duane presiding. Thus it may be said that our judicial system was itinerant from the first.

The legal profession in the early days rated, in the estimation of the public, even lower than the medical. In 1698 Connecticut actually classed lawyers with common drunkards and limited their number to eleven in the whole colony. Rhode Island forbade them to be elected to their House of Deputies. Vermont publicly called them "bandits." In Massachusetts, as late as 1768, only twenty-five men were practicing law and up and down the seaboard it was the same story. But with the establishment of our courts the profession gained in status.

Our circuit judges today travel by plane or motor from court to court, but in the early days no such means was available. Judge Cushing, for example, who rode the circuit in the South had a special four-wheeled phaeton made for himself. It must have been a fancy piece of early carriage-making for we read that it had built-in lockers for his books and storage space for some fancy foods and drinks and mounted on the driver's seat was a jet-black negro with snow-white hair. The judge's wife went along on some of his trips and the story persists that he would read the briefs and she would read the law to him.

The judge, like a great many gentlemen of the period, liked plenty of spice with his whiskey, particularly nutmeg, and in constant fear that the wayside inn might not have any he carried his own supply. It was carried in the vest pocket in a tiny silver box about the size of a modern lady's compact. Several nutmegs were kept in it and the lid had punched through it a number of small, rough-edged holes. When the lid was opened one of the nutmegs could be scraped on the perforations over the whiskey or rum to suit the judge's taste, and he could lean back and contemplate the labors of the day in contentment.

However this picture of placid itineracy may give the wrong impression, for in plain fact the life of a circuit judge must have been anything but easy. While

the young nation was trying to make the course of the justice smooth-going, it did very little to smooth the path of his carriage; the nation's roads were still beyond anything that we can picture. Judge Iredell was not unfair when he complained that his life was not much better than that of a postboy of the period. On some of the roads the use of a carriage was completely out of the question, and in such cases it was back to the saddle horse for the judge. The story is told of Judge Pinckney of Charleston who commonly rode along the highway in company with lawyers and clients, listening to the arguments of each while en route. However if he was called on to give an opinion he insisted on confirming it in writing later and plainly marked the paper "given on circuit." This became so common at one time that it came to be known as "horse-back opinion." The Southern district was considered the worst because the distance between courts was greater than in the North. Judge Iredell, who began this circuit in 1790, wrote that "no Judge can conscientiously undertake to ride the Southern Circuit constantly and perform other parts of his duty . . . I rode upon the last circuit 1900 miles." With the growth of the country the old circuits were broken up into smaller pieces and more and more judges were added. One of the most famous, of course, was Abraham Lincoln of Illinois. To the student of Lincoln the picture of him wearing his tall beaver hat, astride a horse is one of the most appealing we have.

PART IV

PEDDLER'S PROGRESS

12

The Character of the Yankee Peddler

In all that has been said of the character of the Yankee
peddler, little has been complimentary. He has
been maligned by the ministry, the legal profession,
medical men, travelers from abroad, and by plain,
everyday citizens: he was a prime target for anyone
with an ax to grind, and he was seldom on hand to de-
fend himself. In the eighteenth century he was considered a rascal, in the nineteenth he was thought to be
a cheat: he was sharp, crafty, mean, and always on the
lookout for a chance to make a shady deal. In the South
he was the original reason "Damnyankee" became one
word.

The indictments against his character are many. Here
is one by Thomas Hamilton, an English writer of some
reputation in his time, who came here in 1833 and spent
several months traveling and viewing the American
scene to obtain material for a book he was writing to
be called *Men and Manners in America:*

"The whole race of Yankee Peddlers in particular are proverbial for
dishonesty. They go forth annually in the thousands to lie, cog, cheat,
swindle, in short to get possession of their neighbors property in any
manner it can be done with impunity. Their ingenuity in deception is
confessedly very great. They warrent broken watches to be the best
timekeepers in the world; sell pinchbeck trinkets for gold; and always
have a large assortment of wooden nutmegs and stagnant barometers."

And here is what Timothy Dwight said. Dr. Dwight
was no less a person than President of Yale College in
the early part of the nineteenth century and an author
of considerable prominence. In 1823 he published his
Travels in New England and New York and in it he
makes several remarks about the peddlers of the time.
"Many of these young men employed in this business,
part at an early period with both modesty and prin-
ciple. Their sobriety is exchanged for cunning, and
their decent behavior for course impudence." And later
the learned doctor adds, "No course of life tends more
rapidly or more effectually to eradicate every moral
feeling." Another Englishman, who will have to remain nameless since he did not use his by-line, wrote
in an article in the *Penny Magazine of the Society for
the Diffusion of Useful Knowledge,* published in London sometime before 1850:

Even the Americans themselves—possessing a respectable share of self-
esteem—do not estimate very highly the character of their peddlers;
this no doubt due to the many ingenious frauds and deceptions which
some of them have, from time to time, been detected in and yet while
it would be considered a grave misdemeanor in any regular tradesmen
who would attempt the very same species of knavery, yet when a
peddler is detected in having sold you, from the store of his spice box,
wooden nutmegs instead of the true and genuine East Indian article,
instead of any particular odium attaching to him for having cheated
you, you get heartily laughed at for having suffered yourself to be
imposed upon, while he escapes with the fruits of imposition and the
general remark, "I guess it was only a regular Yankee peddler trick."

I doubt that this man had ever actually been sold
any wooden nutmegs. He had probably been cheated
in some other way that was even more deflating to his
ego and simply fell back on the old nutmeg story. It
is doubtful that anybody ever made anything out of
wood that could possibly pass for nutmegs, and if he
did the imitation would cost more than the real thing.
I suspect it is like the old Indian rope trick—everybody
has heard about it but nobody has ever been found who
would step forward and say that he has actually seen
the trick. Smart peddlers undoubtedly knew how to
make good use of their bad reputation as a group by
turning it into an actual advantage. I can imagine some

such approach as this: "Good morning, Madam—I have some beautiful wooden nutmegs here, lady—I will guarantee they are made out of solid *birch;* or maybe you would like some of my hams—they are carved out of the very best *maple*." Such an approach would be almost sure to win an understanding smile from even the most dour of housewives and this would be his opening to display what he really had in his stock.

The fact is that peddlers were so numerous it is impossible for all of them to have been completely honest; and no doubt many a gullible housewife was bilked when she bought some small item from a transient salesman. Naturally, even though there may have been only a few scoundrels in a trade that comprised thousands, the bad actors would make the headlines; a scandalous deal is more interesting to talk about than an ordinary honest one.

No accurate figures on the total number of peddlers exist nor ever have, but many estimates have been made. One authority says that in 1850 there were 10,669 and he follows this up with a figure of 16,595 in 1860. I am inclined to think these figures are low. But if we assume that the number was approximately 17,000 it means that thousands of men were hundreds of miles removed from the restrictions they would have felt in their home areas where they were known—in itself a powerful temptation to palm off a piece of cheap jewelry for a more expensive one. An itinerant, by the very nature of his job, must find it hard to tell the complete truth when a little deviation may mean the difference between sleeping under a roof that night or out under the stars.

Granted, then, a few rascals in the trade could give the whole brotherhood of peddlers a bad reputation—one which their rivals in business could sieze upon and exploit. For as general stores and permanent retail shops came into existence, established merchants had every motive to cast aspersions on transient peddlers who were selling the same goods and services they were, and often more cheaply. Merchants used every means they could think of to keep peddlers out of their communities. One means that the permanent tradesmen and servicemen could use was to demand that every peddler be required to take out a license—for a fee comparable to the taxes that the local merchant had to pay. And in demanding this license the merchants surely would use the argument that the peddler was a suspicious character to be discouraged by any means possible.

In 1841 New York State issued licenses to 302 peddlers; 227 of these carried their stock in trunks and paid a license of $20.00 a year, and 71 paid a little more for the privilege of traveling his route on horseback. No figures are available for the wagon peddlers but we do know that New York was by no means the only state where the merchants with shops talked about the peddler long and loud enough to get their representatives in the local law-making body to pass laws making a license necessary. Pennsylvania, Connecticut, Georgia, Tennessee, Illinois, and Ohio issued licenses and three of these states tried to go further than that— they made it necessary for a peddler to be handicapped or permanently disabled before he could take out a license. This proved very hard to enforce, however, and in practice was more or less ignored.

Since it is natural for settled people to distrust strangers, and merchants had an economic reason for encouraging the attitude, an antagonism grew up—a feeling that the alert peddler was quick to sense and to dodge however he could. A story is told of one peddler who had duly secured his license but did not have it displayed. Sensing a possible shakedown or at least some fun at the expense of the peddler, a local constable approached him just as he arrived at the tavern, bargained with him for several minutes for a Barlow knife and finally paid him a dollar for it. He then demanded that the peddler produce his license, never dreaming the man had one. Of course the peddler whipped out the license and we can imagine the red face of the law. But now the constable was poorer by $1.00 and the owner of a knife he did not want. So, after somewhat recovering from his embarrassment he offered to sell it back to the peddler for half a dollar. This the gentleman of the road promptly accepted.

Thus at that moment the peddler was fifty cents ahead on the whole transaction. But not satisfied with that he made further demands on the law officer because he, the constable, was *selling goods without a license.*

Such stories are probably apocryphal, but they illustrate the attitude toward peddlers that began to exist when they were no longer needed as the sole source of supplies. And while the stories are a credit to the wit and sagacity of the peddler, when they were new they only served to tarnish his name a little more.

A peddler needed a little craft and guile in order to survive against such opposition. He had no union to stand up for him or to lobby for his protection at the state capital. And he lived in an age when there were no public relations counsels to guide him. A Madison Avenue executive could have reshaped the peddler's "image" very effectively. He would have taken one sniff of the very word "peddler" and changed it to something else: "agent" of some sort, just as bowling alleys have become bowling lanes, poolrooms have become pocket-billiard parlors, and false teeth have become dentures. It is to the credit of the peddlers that they managed to live by their wits and sell their products without such modern artifices.

The only fair way to judge the character of the peddler is to look at him against the background of his time. Beyond a few local license requirements and petty ordinances there was virtually no government restraint on business practices; and when we look carefully we find that the peddler as a character comes off rather well when compared with his more respectable settled contemporaries in commerce.

"Let the buyer beware" was a very much more pertinent admonition in the eighteenth and nineteenth centuries than it is now. Benjamin Franklin had coined the expression that "Honesty is the best policy," but the rank and file of businessmen gave evidence that they had either never heard of it or, having heard it, did not believe it. William Beekman, of New York, charged Connecticut businessmen with selling short-weight goods and said, "Seven eighths of the people I have credited in New England have proven to be such damned, ungrateful, cheating fellows that I am now almost afraid to trust any man in Connecticut though he be well recommended from others." And lest you think Mr. Beekman was alone in his opinions let me quote Stephen Collins, a merchant from Philadelphia. He called the merchants of Boston "a pack of deceitful, canting, Presbyterian deacons."

Were things any better in the South? Cotton was sold by the pound and the temptation to add to the weight of a bale by putting stones inside it was more than many shippers could withstand. Shortly before the Civil War the records show that at one time the docks of Liverpool were piled high with thousands of bales of cotton from America that had been so thoroughly sanded that no English mill could be found to buy any of it at any price.

Land in the Middle West sold all the way from 1 cent to as high as $1.25 per acre. What are we supposed to think of white men who would buy thousands of acres from the Indians for a bottle of bad whiskey and a string of cheap beads?

Some of the big fur dealers of the early days, for example the ones whose descendants became part of the 400 of New York society, commonly paid the Indians for a big load of beaver fur with a hat full of trinkets such as can be bought at a five and dime store today. Richardson Wright in his *Hawkers and Walkers in Early America* put it this way: "Were some of the great fur merchants of early America alive and carrying on their business today in their accustomed way, the Atlanta and Fort Leavenworth prisons would be nowhere near big enough to hold them."

Many of the suppliers of the army gave a shining example of normal business practice in the Civil War. A new term had to be invented for a textile invented by some of our larger clothing manufacturers—it was "shoddy." This was made from old rags shredded into bits and rewoven into cloth for the Army Blues. It would fall apart on the slightest provocation. And army boots made largely of paper sold at many hundreds per cent quick profit to the makers.

As for the suppliers of meat for the soldiers: for years after the war, people living along the National

Road told stories of the sickening odor that hung in the atmosphere days after the passage of a wagon train-load of filthy, diseased meat from Chicago headed for the army quartermaster.

And as for guns, although this is hard to believe now, one arms manufacturer shipped an order of 10,000 new guns to a Union camp in the East. For some reason the receiving officers insisted on test-firing several guns out of the shipment. *Not one* of those tested would even shoot and the entire lot was quite rightly returned to the manufacturer. However, the manufacturer was not left holding the guns: He did not hang his head in shame nor do his best to correct the faults in the guns. He merely sold them to General Fremont's hard-pressed troops in Missouri.

Profiteering in meat flourished during the Civil War but did not end with it. In Chicago, in the years following the war, the four largest meat packers realized how wasteful competitive bidding could be—for them. It would be much more economical if they did not bid against each other for the cattle and hogs that were brought into the market by farmers. A sort of arrangement was made. As Stewart Holbrook put it, "There was no perceptible conspiracy; only a fortuitous harmony of minds." When the cattle and hogs were brought into the Union Stockyards only four buyers would appear. The first offered a low price; the second was not interested; the third, after wrinkling his nose, showed no disposition to buy; the fourth yawned and said he was in no hurry. The next day, almost the same thing would take place, except that the buyers assumed different, prearranged roles. Of course the cattle finally went at the lowest possible price; and the practice went on for several years, with enormous losses to the farmers and correspondingly high profits to the meat packers.

In 1898 during the Spanish American War another meat scandal occurred fully as bad as those in the Civil War. Holbrook describes it this way: "To say that the condition of much of this meat was 'bad' was arrant flattery. It was rotten. At a training camp at Chicka-mauga, for instance, wagon loads of beef arriving from

Chicago could be trailed through the camp by the live maggots that were shaken off and fell to the ground."

Daniel Drew, who was to become a Wall Street operator along with Jay Gould and Jim Fisk, was also engaged in a meat racket when he was a young man, but he had a different angle: he sold it on the hoof. He was a buyer and seller of cattle and spent much of his time walking from farm to farm in Pennsylvania and Ohio. When he had collected something like a thousand head of cattle he would turn back toward New York over the route that is now the Pennsylvania Turnpike, driving the herd ahead of him. When they were near New York he always managed to have a few barrels of salt on the wagon, and out they came; the heads of the barrels were knocked in and the salt spread around. The cattle, which had been kept on a salt-free diet for several days, would lick it up ravenously. By some strange coincidence all this would happen right beside a river or pond of fresh water. The reason

Daniel Drew started the Erie Railroad stock fraud. *New York Public Library.*

was obvious. A gallon of water weighs nearly eight pounds and I imagine those cattle could drink more than a gallon apiece: one gallon is eight pounds and if he had 1,000 head of cattle—yes, young Mr. Drew would do all right when he sold that herd at so much per hundred pounds. When you hear the term "watered stock" these days, think of Daniel Drew; he did not coin the word himself of course but he certainly was the inspiration for it.

Daniel Drew was later to become a principal figure in the Erie Panic, a business scandal that illustrates the methods used by our tycoons of the nineteenth century and makes the peccadilloes attributed to the humble peddler seem trifling indeed.

With Jay Gould and Jim Fisk (a former peddler of tinware) Drew controlled the Erie Railroad, which connected New York with Lake Erie. The New York Central and Hudson River Railroad, which ran from New York to Buffalo, was controlled by Commodore Vanderbilt who took a dim view of the Erie's competition and publicly announced his intention of taking it over. His agents bought Erie stock wherever they could find it, and it soon looked as if the Commodore was close to gaining control of his competition. But then, mysteriously, a new issue of Erie stock appeared on the market, and the Commodore was forced to buy some more. The more stock he bought, the more appeared, just as fast as Messrs. Drew, Fisk, and Gould could have it printed.

The Commodore, who had a number of public officials on his payroll, got his friend Judge Barnard, who was one of the prominent figures in the notorious Boss Tweed gang, to issue an injunction against the printing of any more Erie stock. Jay Gould answered this by obtaining a counterinjunction, and the presses rolled on turning out Erie stock—100,000 more shares. The Commodore had the judge issue a warrant for the arrest of Gould, Fisk, and Drew and an order stating that the Erie Railroad was bankrupt; the judge was careful to name a receiver favored by the Commodore.

By this time, Gould, Fisk, and Drew had collected

Jay Gould, another Erie conspirator, confers with W.A.H. Loveland. *New York Public Library.*

some six million dollars in cash from the sale of worthless Erie stock; they packed it into suitcases and headed for the New Jersey ferry, with a gang of fifty hired thugs to protect their getaway. The Commodore sent a gang of so-called deputy sheriffs to the ferry, and there was a pitched battle between them and the Erie "detectives" at the ferry slip, during which the three principals managed to get their suitcases of currency across the river into the more friendly atmosphere of New Jersey. Ordinarily New Jersey is just as law-abiding a state as New York, but in this case, instead of the New Jersey authorities meeting the fleeing bandits armed with warrants, they escorted the three to the Hotel Taylor in Jersey City and placed an armed guard around them for their protection. The Erie men actually mounted three cannons on the dock in Jersey City and provided four lifeboats carrying twelve armed men each as a shore patrol, to keep the Vanderbilt deputies away.

When interviewed in "Fort Taylor" by reporters from the *Herald,* the *Times,* the *Post,* and the *Tribune,* Jim Fisk said: "Commodore Vanderbilt owns New York. He owns the Stock Exchange, the New York streets and the railroad. We are ambitious young men. We saw there was no chance for us to expand in your city, so we came over here to Jersey to grow up with the country."

After staying several weeks in "Fort Taylor" Jay Gould packed half a million dollars in a suitcase and went to Albany, where he is said to have "assiduously cultivated members of the legislature," which is to say that he handed out fistfuls of money to those who fa-

Commodore Vanderbilt opposed Drew, Fisk and Gould. *New York Public Library.*

vored him in his contest with Vanderbilt. He wanted the legislature to legalize what he had already done by converting Erie Railroad bonds into stock. At that time Boss Tweed was a state senator and to no one's surprise he worked hand in glove with Gould, lining up the legislators on the side of "justice." Vanderbilt too was in Albany with a checkbook, although he did not say just how much money he distributed. Gould spent about a million dollars and won the day, so we may assume that Vanderbilt's gratuities were not as lavish as Gould's. The victory seems to have gone to the highest bidder.

The public loved the whole affair; there was no great hue and cry for the arrest of the Erie conspirators. We may suppose that anyone who was left holding worthless Erie securities did not like it, but for the most part it was all a hilarious sideshow. No one was punished; in fact these men were heroes to the public; they were not crooks, but merely smart operators; and they were accepted by the best people and became members of the aristocracy.

The same people who applauded the canniness of Gould, Fisk, and Drew were no doubt the first to accuse the plodding peddler who sold a patent medicine that was as harmless as it was useless or a clock that would not keep time. Against the background of his age, the lowly peddler does not seem to be quite the crafty villain he has grown to be in legend. No doubt there were dishonest peddlers; they never made the headlines, never were discussed or admired in the taverns in the streets. And if some peddlers were dishonest, they had towering examples, such as Gould, Fisk, and Drew, to follow: if a Fisk or a Tweed could openly rob the public and live in luxury and esteem, why should a peddler have had any more conscience about selling a cheap clock for more than its value or passing off a worthless (and probably very comforting) cough medicine?

We will have to grant that some peddlers were unscrupulous (Fisk as a tinware peddler probably learned some of his tricks on the road, although his crookedness was probably more a personal character trait than a typical peddler's trick), but when we consider their

JIM FISK

situation it seems more likely that most peddlers were reasonably honest. Half of them were independent salesmen who owned their entire stock and could dispose of it as they saw fit; but the other half were staked by some manufacturer or wholesaler, who must have considered them reliable if they entrusted them with wagonloads of goods that might be worth as much as $2,000 per wagon. Most of the peddlers were young men looking for a place to settle down as merchants and solid citizens; if conscience did not restrain them from dishonest dealings good sense would. Others plied the same routes year after year, and would not want to blacken their names in growing communities that they might visit again. And still others—those with foresight and ambition and industry—became the backbone of the nation's commerce once they established a business and made it grow; some of our largest and most respectable enterprises were founded by peddlers.

So it is safe to assume that a majority of the peddlers were reliable in a commonplace, everyday sort of way for which no one would remember them; while a few scoundrels brought disrepute to the whole brotherhood through their shady deals. Even at their worst the peddlers were only pennysnatchers, but the great financiers were pirates.

13

From Peddler to
Big Business Man

In the early 1800's and far into the century, no college or university offered any courses in business or finance; you learned about business just by engaging in it. The "hard knocks" school of peddling seems to have served remarkably well as a training-ground for many different kinds of business, if we can judge from the men who graduated from its ranks; and many of the big enterprises that serve us today had their origins in a lowly peddler's route.

Many of the early peddlers won renown for other things than peddling. Benedict Arnold, for example, although we hardly think of him as a credit to the profession, spent the years of his youth peddling woolen goods up and down the Hudson Valley, through the very same area where he later operated as a military man and betrayed George Washington. He was a brilliant man and might have had an honorable career in business if he had kept away from the army.

Everyone has heard of the Worcester Polytechnic Institute, one of the finest schools in the country; but not many know of its founder, John Boynton, who made a fortune peddling tinware and thus was able to endow the school. And if Abraham Lincoln had not become President, we would not know, as scholars tell us now, that his father was a part-time peddler. When

the elder Lincoln decided to leave Kentucky for
Indiana he acquired a trunk full of small notions to
peddle along the way—a common practice in the nineteenth century when travelers wished to offset the expense of a trip.

We remember John Fitch as one of the early inventors of the steamboat: his model had six oars standing straight up on each side of the boat, with a steam
operated crank to lift the oars, dip them in the water,
and push them backward to propel the boat. But long
before he developed this idea, he had engaged in many
trades, including peddling. Fitch was something of a
genius and a "rolling stone" as well. Born in Windsor,
Connecticut, in 1743, he was successively an itinerant
clock repairman, traveling through much of New
York, Connecticut, and New Jersey for several years;
then a manufacturer of brass buttons; then a silversmith; a gunsmith during the Revolution; a brewer of
beer; a surveyor; a maker of maps; and, finally, the
inventor of a steamboat that actually ran for several
years between Burlington, New Jersey, and Philadelphia.

Fitch's steamboat attempt to duplicate the action of human paddlers.

About eight of his younger years he spent repairing clocks through the countryside until he arrived at Trenton, New Jersey, where he set up a shop to repair clocks and to make brass buttons. Apparently he could not get enough customers to come to his shop so he took to the road again, this time with a stock of brass buttons he had made in his shop. The records indicate that in two weeks he had sold out his buttons at a good profit and repaired twelve clocks.

Back to Trenton he went, determined to go into the button business on a large scale. First he scoured the surrounding countryside for all the old brass kettles and pots and pans he could find; there must have been plenty, because he hired twenty men to work in his plant while he himself continued to peddle the output. A little while later he added silver buttons to his line to make it more complete. Old records indicate he did very well on this venture until the Revolution broke in on his plans. He had somewhat more than eight hundred pounds stowed away when the war came along to interfere.

He promptly joined Washington's army as a lieutenant but on his plea that he could manufacture guns for the army he was released. Fitch set to work seriously to make guns and is supposed actually to have produced a few, but the British discovered his factory and promptly destroyed all his equipment. Shortly after this he turned up in Valley Forge, not at all as a half-starved soldier dressed in rags and without shoes, but as a well dressed beer salesman. He probably made the beer himself, perhaps with the help of one or two others (the making of beer was a very common accomplishment at that time in many homes and its consumption was even more common). At any rate he is supposed to have made a net profit of about five pounds a barrel.

The records become a little hazy at this point, as, before the war was over, we find him back in the business of making brass and silver buttons. And in 1780 he turned up in Kentucky as a surveyor (no end to his abilities, apparently). A party of Indians working with the British captured him and took him to Canada as a prisoner. While there he made some clocks out of wood and more buttons to sell to the Canadians. Eventually he was exchanged and went back to the Kentucky area to do some more surveying. During this time the Northwest Territory had been set up by the new Congress and Fitch saw that maps of it would be in demand. So he managed to make one, and with a huge bundle of 800 copies of it he peddled them house-to-house at a handsome profit. When he had sold all his maps he went back East, apparently with the intention of settling down and putting down some roots. He had built a little home for himself on the Delaware River, and he used to spend hours every day looking at the sailboats going up and down stream whenever there was a breeze to supply the power. His mind eventually rebelled at the idea of a shipload of valuable merchandise lying becalmed for hours waiting for a breeze to come up, so he set to work to find a way to apply the newly discovered power of steam to navigation. Apparently he started his experiments from scratch, knowing nothing about the work of others on the same problem; but he was never able to protect the design that he developed in 1787 because it infringed on other inventions.

Giving up here, he went to France where he had no success either, so back to America he came, settling this time in Kentucky. But success was not to be his, for in a fit of despondency he took his own life, in 1790, when he was fifty-five years old.

Big, handsome Jim Fisk, whom we have already encountered as a railroad tycoon of dubious morality, also came up from the ranks of the peddlers. He was born in Pownal, Vermont, the son of a fairly successful tin peddler who wanted Jim to take over one of his several wagons as soon as the boy was old enough. But Jim had other ideas, ideas which were to shape his career—he ran away with a traveling circus. By this time P. T. Barnum was teaching the world the uses of publicity, and while Jim's employer was not Barnum he had evidently learned something about showmanship from him, because Jim came home well-versed in the art of circus publicity or ballyhoo which he was later to apply in all his business operations. He had found out that villages, towns and cities could be "taken" if properly approached, that people were willing to believe anything if you talked loud enough.

So when his father finally persuaded him to take a wagon out on the road Jim adopted some of the ideas he had acquired in the circus. There were hundreds of tin peddlers on the highways then, and Jim knew that he would be just one more of them if he did not do something to distinguish himself. So he borrowed the circus idea of advance billing. He had his wagon painted in gay colors and hung with bunting and flags; bells jingled on his horses; and he dressed himself in a

Cartoons of the improbable rascal, Jim Fisk. *New York Public Library.*

smart-looking black silk suit, shiny boots up to his knees, and the largest and whitest cowboy hat he could find. He had handbills and posters printed with a picture of him and his wagon, and hired a boy to go ahead of him a week or so in advance to put the posters up all over town and pass out the handbills; and, whenever he could find a few men that could toot a horn or play some kind of instrument, he had them on hand when his wagon rolled into the village square on a Saturday afternoon or some other holiday.

Jim had learned a valuable thing—people prefer to deal with people they *know,* or at least people that they have heard of before, rather than somebody completely unknown to them. In a day when reading material was hard to find they would read the posters over and over again. By the time Jim arrived in town in his gaudy getup, he already seemed a familiar figure. He perfected his technique as he went along and sold a vast amount of tinware. Year after year he increased his sales and his personal popularity, and became so skilled at what we now call merchandising that the big Boston store, Jordan, Marsh Company, offered him a vice-presidency in 1860.

Jim was to peddle all his life; when he left Jordan, Marsh to go into Wall Street he changed from retail goods to railroads, and along with Daniel Drew and Jay Gould he made enough money to fill every tin pan on his old wagon with gold.

Railroads were expanding so profitably at this time that it is not surprising that many ambitious young men were drawn to them from the ranks of peddlers, the school of future magnates. Collis Potter Huntington, best remembered today as the genius of the Southern Pacific and Central Pacific Railroads, later as a collector of fine art and rare books, and still later as the founder of The Mariners' Museum in Newport News, Virginia, began his fabulous career as a peddler right in Poverty Hollow, Connecticut, where he was born early in the nineteenth century. By doing odd jobs in the area near his father's farm he managed to accumulate $175 and with this security he set up a credit with New York merchants for $3,000. According to his biographer, Cerinda W. Evans, he bought a stock of watch findings, jewelry, silverware, needles, knives, tape, thread, and combs. He carried his wares in two tin boxes that were about two feet long and sixteen inches deep. He carried one in each hand using a shoulder strap for additional support. Selling these, he invested in a packhorse and he was off again with a bigger assortment. Soon even a sturdy packhorse could not carry all the goods he wanted and he bought a wagon. At about this time, according to Evans, he added a new service, the buying, at handsome discounts, of notes that had been taken in payment for clocks and other goods by many of his fellow peddlers. This must have been a risky venture when we consider how widely scattered the makers were and how easy it was for a settler to pull up stakes and move into the next state, leaving no forwarding address. The records give no figures on this department of the young man's business but all the facts that have come down to us indicate that he was just as successful in his collections as he was in his sale of goods.

But after a few years of this peddling during which he became intimately acquainted with very large areas of the East and South he decided to leave the road and

Collis P. Huntington began his career as a peddler. *Brown Brothers.*

become a merchant. He selected a store in Oneonta, New York, and you can be sure his selection of goods sprang directly from his years of contact with the pioneers. But in 1849 the recent discovery of gold in California struck the young men of the whole country like an avalanche, carrying everyone with it. Almost daily, groups of young men were organizing parties and starting for the West Coast with high hopes and, all too frequently, little else. Young Mr. Huntington was no exception to the gold fever but his methods were very different. He bought a large assortment of tools and hardware such as he knew would be needed in a mining area and shipped them to himself in Sacramento. Then he took passage on a ship for Panama where he planned somehow to walk across the isthmus in hopes of finding a ship on the western side that would carry him to California.

But the little fever-ridden town of Chagres where the ship landed him on the East Coast almost proved his downfall as it did in fact to hundreds of other gold-seeking passengers from his ship and several others crowded into the port waiting for some means of crossing the isthmus. Digging into his experience peddling with packhorses, he bought the only animal available, a donkey, and made arrangements with other passengers who were willing to pay a handsome sum for transporting their goods through the jungles to the other side. For a period of several months he found himself in the business of carrying freight and guiding gold-seekers. He made twelve trips on foot, twelve round trips, with the net result that when he finally landed in San Francisco the $1,200 cash he had started out with had increased to more than $5,000 over and above the entire expense of his long trip.

Another railroad magnate who used a peddler's technique to sell railroad stock was William Butler Ogden; unlike the other big businessmen who graduated from the ranks, Ogden resorted to peddling as a means for accomplishing his aim.

Ogden's family, in New York, was fairly well to do. In a moment of what must have been regarded by most sensible people as sheer hysteria they had invested $100,000 in Chicago real estate. At the time, Chicago had been incorporated as a town for just two years and consisted of one hundred eighty people living in forty-three wretched shanties and cabins in a swamp over-grown with weeds and wild onions: most of the citizens operated dives of some kind or sold real estate which must have looked rather unpromising. Nearby Michigan City was a dozen times as large and Milwaukee was twice as big. So when Ogden, in 1835, at the age of thirty, got off the stagecoach on what is now Lake Street, he looked about him and wrote to his family, "You have been guilty of the greatest folly."

His idea in coming to Chicago was simply to unload the acreage for whatever he could get and count himself lucky no matter what the sum was. He had his land surveyed and laid out in lots, and then announced an auction. To his surprise, dozens of people showed up with fistfuls of money and bought lots by fives and tens. Ogden said he thought they must have been affected by swamp fever. In three or four days he had back the $100,000 investment and found that fully two thirds of the acreage still belonged to him. He returned to New York to give his family the money, then came back to Chicago a few months later to see what could be done with the rest of the land.

By this time half a dozen new streets had been laid out, a few dozen more shanties built, and the price of land had tripled since his auction. He sold off the balance of his acreage at a tremendous profit and went into business for himself. Two years later he was mayor of Chicago. Ten years later, with the city growing by leaps and bounds, Ogden thought it should have a railroad. But here he ran into opposition; unbelievable as it now seems, many citizens opposed the idea, arguing that Chicago should be a retail town where farmers could come with a load of produce to sell and then spend their money. If there was a railroad the farmer would ship his produce in and never come to town.

A railroad required higher financing than even Ogden could manage; and besides money he needed the support of the farmers of the surrounding area. And so he became a peddler. He got himself a horse and buggy and set out on a long trip through northern Illinois, selling stock in his Galena and Chicago Union Railroad. In a few months he had sold $250,000 worth of it. In 1848 the first train steamed proudly into Chicago and the railroad, now the Chicago and Northwestern, was a tremendous success.

It was to Ogden, now a big capitalist, that Cyrus Hall McCormick, the inventor and builder of the reaper, went when he needed money to improve his machine. McCormick, whose invention made the Midwest the breadbasket of the nation, was also a peddler of sorts. For many years he peddled his reapers from farm to farm, listening to the farmers' needs and making improvements in his product. When he could foresee a widespread demand for his machine he asked

Cyrus P. McCormick.

Ogden for $25,000 to open a plant in Chicago; Ogden gave it to him and the company became McCormick, Ogden and Co. They sold reapers to farmers at a fixed price, payable $30.00 down and the balance of $90.00 over a six-month period. Knowing farmers well as a result of his peddling experience, McCormick realized that a bad crop year would keep them from paying; but as he knew most of them were honest he made allowances for crop failures in fixing his terms.

Among inventors, mechanics, architects, and builders the name of Stanley Tools is known and respected. Its giant tool and hardware plants dominate the skylines of New Britain, Connecticut, and many other towns. Its founder was Frederick Trenck Stanley, who was born in New Britain in 1802, of a family that had settled there in the 1600's. He grew up in New Britain like any other lad of his time, finished school when he was sixteen, and started looking around to see what he could do to earn a living. Normally he might have been expected to become an apprentice in one of the town's small shops, the harness-makers, or one of the new carriage-making shops that were just getting started. But (and how modern it sounds) a depression was on

McCORMICK REAPER

—the War of 1812 had just closed—and in a vain effort to prevent our people from becoming manufacturers England was sending over shiploads of goods and almost giving them away; and our importers were buying them too.

As a result the many small manufacturers in New Britain were having a hard time merely staying in business, let alone hiring inexperienced lads like Fred Stanley. So Fred trudged down to New Haven where his likable smile and ready tongue found him a clerk's job in a store. It was what later was to be called a general store—they sold nails and pickles, yard goods and rope, spices and rum—in fact just about anything they could get and sell. New Haven was accessible by boat at the time and to a limited extent by heavy wagons on the Post Road so that a general store there was feasible. The young man stayed there five years, getting a practical knowledge of meeting people and selling goods that was to be priceless to him later.

During this time his father died at sea, leaving Fred a little money which was to become his when he reached the age of twenty-one. He could have opened a store right in New Haven where by that time he had built a wide acquaintance, or he could have gone back to New Britain where there were enough Stanleys to keep a young man in business.

But he did neither—he became a peddler. Not out of New Britain—instead he went down to Fayetteville, North Carolina. He picked Fayetteville because the town was on a river, about eighty miles from the coast or about as far upstream as boats could go. Small coastwise ships could pick up manufactured goods of all kinds in New England ports and go on down the coast, go up the Cape Fear River and unload in Fayetteville. It was therefore the trading center for all of western North Carolina, eastern Tennessee, and southwestern Virginia.

In the 1820's Yankee manufacturers were fast adopting the method of shipping south to some such center by boat (or even by Conestoga wagons as the roads improved), setting up a store there not only to take care of the townspeople, but also, by running peddler wagons out of the store in all directions, to take care of the farmers who were too busy on the farm to struggle all the way into town to buy supplies.

Stanley sailed for Fayetteville with a stock of New England goods of all kinds; he probably obtained much of it on credit in New Britain and New Haven where he was well known. He set up his own business and peddled from a wagon in the back country for the next three years, and it was during this time that he learned what people needed. Among the many items he sold was hardware: for example, iron hinges to replace the leather ones on settlers' cabin doors. Stanley usually had actually to install the hinges to prove they were better than the leather ones.

As Constable Dogberry said,

Comparisons are Odorous!

Look here, upon this picture,

Then on *this*.

The counterfeit presentment of two hinges!

See what a grace is seated on this brow.
A combination and a form indeed
Where every god did seem to set his seal,
To give the world assurance of a hinge.
This is Stanley's Corrugated Steel Hinge.

Look you now what follows.
The Ancient,
Like a mildewed ear,
Blasting his wholesome brother.

Ha! Have you eyes and judgment?
But what judgment would step from
This   to   *This?*

When you can have, at no more cost, **The Corrugated,** will you still use **The Ancient?** What devil is't that thus hath cozen'd you at hoodman-blind?

FOR FURTHER PARTICULARS ADDRESS

THE STANLEY WORKS, Sole Manufacturers of The Corrugated.

NEW BRITAIN CONN, or 79 CHAMBERS ST., NEW YORK.

In 1826 he sold out his business at a nice profit and returned to New Britain to set up a factory to make tools and hardware. He now had a backlog of experience that was invaluable to him. He knew what settlers needed and bought; and he knew what he could have sold if he had had it to sell. Like many other peddlers of his time he came home to supply the market he had discovered as a traveler. It is probable that much of the dominance in the manufacture of small items that Connecticut now enjoys is primarily due to the impact of the army of peddlers on their return to the home-town.

Another eastern small-town boy whose Yankee in-genuity and peddling experience made him a million-aire was B. T. Babbitt, who became a soap manufac-turer. Born in western New York in 1809, son of a blacksmith, he lived eighty years, in the course of which he not only made a fortune for himself but also showed his competitors how to do it; the company he founded is now in its second century and still going strong.

Ben's peddling career came about because he found himself with a supply of something to sell. His first business venture at the age of fourteen determined the course of his life. The distillery in his hometown kept several hundred hogs, fed on mash, in the yard next door. One day someone carelessly threw out a pile of mash so hot that a couple of hogs were badly burned and had to be killed. Young Babbitt bought the dead hogs for $13.90, salvaged the edible meat, and made soap out of the fat. There was nothing new about this; every farmer made soap out of fat of all kinds, using wood ashes from the fireplace for that purpose. But it happened that Ben's soap was unusually good and he sold it. The next thing he did was to persuade some farmers not to make their own soap—let him make soap for them in return for their hogs. Eventually he made enough satisfactory deals with farmers to pro-cure supplies, and peddled his own soap around the area until he was eighteen years old. Then he moved down to New York City, where he set up a factory on Washington Street, making soap and adding a few other items to his line.

At this point he did two things that revolutionized the soap business; they were so sound that soap-makers are still following the practice. Before Babbitt, all soap was made in bars up to a yard long; the dealer simply cut off half a pound or whatever the customer ordered. Babbitt cut his bars into convenient-sized cakes and wrapped them in an attractive paper cover with his name on each one—"identification of the source" is what Madison Avenue men call this today. He charged a little more for this feature and when some people balked at the price, he introduced the premium method of merchandising—giving away some useful article for the return of a few of his soap wrappers. This is familiar enough to us now, but at the time it was a sensational innovation. Once again the peddler's knowledge of what buyers want led to improvements in manufacturing and selling goods.

When Dick Sears was sixteen, up in the little town of Spring Valley, Minnesota, his father died and left the family almost penniless. His father was a Civil War veteran and had been a blacksmith all his life. Faced with the problem of earning a living Dick decided he wanted to be a telegrapher and after months of hard work he qualified. Being a telegrapher in the latter half of the nineteenth century was the aim of many young men; there was something dramatic about it; you could cock your ear and listen to a lot of dots and dashes coming over the wires that was just an unintelligible lot of noise to everybody else but you. You could assume a bored expression, maybe stifle a couple of yawns, and then say, "That guy is getting slower all the time—I nearly go to sleep when he is talking," and covertly look around to see how many bystanders were impressed. Yes, the telegrapher's job had a lot of glamor to it in those days, so we cannot blame Dick for liking it. He did so well with it that before long he was made station agent at the Minneapolis and St. Louis Railway station in North Redwood, Minnesota.

The duties of being a station agent in a tiny town did not demand too much of his time and he found he

RICHARD W. SEARS

Richard W. Sears, at the age of 23.

in his capacity of station agent, told the local jeweler
about their arrival but for some reason that is not clear
at this time the merchant refused to accept the shipment at all. The watches could have been faulty in the
opinion of the local man, they might have been too
high priced for his trade, or he may already have had
a stock of watches larger than he needed. I suppose we
will never know, but whatever the reason was, their
refusal by that jeweler was the turning point in the life
of young Sears.

Young Dick had the vision and imagination that
make a good salesman; he envisioned selling those
could add to his income by selling lumber and coal
to the local people (we can be sure he never suspected
it at the time but *selling* was to be the main work of his
long and useful life).

After a few years of this activity a shipment of
watches arrived in his station from a Chicago manufacturer. They were consigned to a local store. Dick,
watches to every station agent on his railroad. He found

he could buy the whole shipment for a small sum and make a fine big profit on every one of them. He promptly bought them and went to work peddling them up and down the line. Before they were gone he ordered more of them, moved them out in no time, and ordered still more.

Naturally, before long, the job of station agent became less attractive to him than the watch business and so he set up the R. W. Sears Watch Company in Minneapolis. Only a year later he gave up the Minneapolis store and opened up in teeming Chicago. By this time he had hired and trained salesmen to go out and sell watches in the way that he knew so well how to do.

But even spark plugs like Dick Sears have their troubles and his was watches that did not watch, so to speak—that refused to keep even reasonably accurate time or even to run. He desperately needed a watch repairman who could be counted on now and then to come up with a miracle in the way of watch repairing. Lady Luck was still with the young man because a young chap from Indiana named Alvah C. Roebuck answered his advertisement and was hired.

Thus from the humble peddler of watches in the small towns of Minnesota grew the gigantic business of Sears Roebuck & Co.

——————◆——————

GREAT ATLANTIC AND PACIFIC TEA COMPANY

PEDDLERS OF FOOD

Peddlers of food and beverages were not so numerous in the early days of America as peddlers of hard goods, since a man traveling afoot or on horseback could not carry bulky or perishable commodities. Coffee was still almost unknown in England and the colonies and tea was just being tried out in London. About the only foodstuffs a peddler could carry in the 1600's were spices, sugar, and salt.

The common beverages were cider and rum; water and milk were unsanitary and people drank them as little as possible. But some time before 1700 a new beverage was added: rum from the West Indies. Rum

is made from molasses, and it did not take the thrifty
Yankees long to find out that they could save money by
importing the molasses from Barbados and distilling it
in New England. By the middle of the eighteenth century no fewer than fifteen distilleries were operating
in the Boston area, and the price per gallon for the
best rum was under two shillings. Peddlers could not
carry much of it until roads and wagons came into use,
but then the wagonloads began rolling out of New
England bearing huge quantities. It sold then in Boston for one shilling and in eastern New York and western Pennsylvania for any price the conscience of the
peddler dictated. It was shipped in barrels and kegs
and even hogsheads containing a hundred gallons.
These were commonly sold to the tavern-keeper or the
general store, where they were set up on a platform and
tapped with a spigot. So the most common beverages
of Colonial days were alcoholic. John Adams wrote,
"If the ancients drank wine as our people drink rum
and cider, it is no wonder we hear of so many possessed
with devils." Yet he himself to the end of his long life
always began the day with a tankard of hard cider.

By the middle of the eighteenth century tea and
coffee were common beverages wherever they were
available—that is, in the seaport cities—and by the
time wagons could travel the road the peddler saw the
sale possibilities in them and added them to his load of
rum. Coffee in those days was not what it is now—a
blend of several kinds. Today's coffee-packer sets his
own standard of taste and mixes together a dozen or
more types of green coffee, making allowances for
variations in flavor. But in early America, coffee was
just coffee; a shipload arrived consisting of several
hundred bags from different plantations, each with its
own peculiar flavor. A sample from each might be
brewed and the price per pound set on the bag according to the taste of the importer; then out it went to the
coffee houses of the coast and the retail stores in the
larger cities. But throughout the greater part of the
young nation the peddler in his wagon was the only
means of bringing it to the table of the settler. He

bought it in fifty pound bags at maybe 4 cents a pound and sold it to the consumer five hundred miles inland for 8 or 10 cents. He might carry two kinds, one low priced and another somewhat dearer for the more discriminating, and who was to say that they might not have been scooped out of the same bag or barrel? The coffee sold by the peddler throughout nearly all of the nineteenth century was green and, of course, unground. You roasted your own in a tin pan or in a specially built tin roaster that the tinware manufacturers designed.

In the northern colonies and states, the only natural sweets were honey and maple syrup; sugar cane was a product of the West Indies, although a good deal was raised in Louisiana in the nineteenth century. New York was the principal port of entry for cane; before the Revolution there were three small refineries in lower Manhattan and by 1800 a dozen of them were in business. They produced not the fine white granulated sugar we have today, but a hard brown lumpy sugar, which when broken up looked so much like sand that it became a common practice in the sugar business to mix sand with it, and perhaps some peddlers were guilty of this practice although it could not long go undetected.

Salt was not quite so scarce since there were many deposits of it here; they were discovered in the eighteenth century in western New York, Michigan, and eastern Ohio. Men sometimes discovered salt deposits by following the trails of animals. Sea water could be evaporated but it was a long process and the resulting product was impure and unpalatable. Salt was of course indispensable to the pioneer for flavoring food; but it had an additional importance for the preservation of food. There were very few ways of keeping food open to our ancestors. Meat could be preserved by drying it in the sun, but much of it could spoil in the process; certain kinds could be smoked. Some fruits and vegetables could be preserved by drying; and in the South peaches were preserved by covering them with corn whiskey, which also enhanced their flavor. Pickling was known but this too required salt. Food could best be kept by putting it in a strong solution of brine or rubbing it with dry salt. So the wagon peddler carrying salt was indispensable to settlers in remote places.

Of course from the earliest times the peddler carried spices. Pepper, nutmeg, cloves, and ginger were the most common, and very valuable. In the Middle Ages a pound of ginger was worth a sheep while a pound of mace brought three sheep; cloves cost the equivalent of $20.00 a pound. Pepper was so valuable that it was counted out one peppercorn at a time. Down to Elizabethan times the sailors and guards on London docks had to have their pockets sewn up to prevent them smuggling in spices. By Colonial times the cost of spices had come down, but they were still dear, and England controlled the trade until the nineteenth century when the Yankee clipper ship came into use. Then Jonathan Carnes, a Yankee skipper out of Salem, Massachusetts, brought in a whole shipload of pepper and made a profit of over 700 per cent on it. This was unusual, but it served to make Salem the chief port of entry for spices for some years. The peddler would seldom be able to buy spices at the dockside; usually an importer would buy whole wagonloads, and the peddler would go to him for his spices, which were weighed out of their canisters with a steelyard.

In the early days the foodstuffs a peddler could carry were luxury items; but when tea and coffee became common beverages they formed the staple items in a grocer's stock, and many a grocery business was built on them. The most outstanding is of course the Great Atlantic and Pacific Tea Company.

The A&P is now a great chain of supermarkets all over America; but two generations ago many a housewife thought of it as a wagon that stopped at her door with an assortment of tea, coffee, spices, and extracts. The driver had a pleasant good-morning for her and perhaps a bit of gossip. He was a peddler exactly like many other wagon salesmen who were to be found by the hundreds all over the country wherever there were roads, but he dealt only in A&P products. And although the A&P was not started as an itinerant peddling operation, for many years up to 1910 it sent out its salesmen to the customers as well as attracting customers to its permanent stores. It had its beginnings over a century ago and was the creation of George H. Hartford and his two sons George and John.

George H. Hartford was born in Augusta, Maine, in 1833. His boyhood was probably much the same as any other boy's of his time; he went to school, tried his hand at a few jobs around his hometown, went out to St. Louis for a few weeks, then came back to New York. He was twenty-six then, and he had an idea that was to have a profound effect on American retail business.

In 1859—it was the year John Brown was hanged at Harpers Ferry, the Comstock Lode was discovered in Nevada, and the first oil well was brought in—George Hartford tried out his idea. At that time tea was the most popular table beverage in America despite its high cost. It came from the Orient by huge clipper ships across the Pacific, around the Horn, and north by the Atlantic to New York. On the docks it was bought by importers, who in turn sold it to wholesalers, who resold it to stores or to peddlers. This added up to three price markups before the tea arrived in the home of the consumer.

To the Yankee mind of young George this situation sounded like opportunity. Why not buy a whole shipload of tea just as the ship tied up at the pier and sell it right on the dock directly to the consumers at a price far below what the housewife would have to pay if the tea had to go through all the usual channels?

Little is known today of the details of this operation

other than the fact that he sold out the first shipload at a price only about one-third what the housewife would have had to pay under normal circumstances at that time. We also know, however, that he made a profit, because he continued selling tea for the rest of his life. But we can assume that the sale at dockside did not go quite as fast as he had hoped for, because the housewife was obliged to leave her normal shopping area to go down to the pier. George saw this point and immediately did something about it.

P. T. Barnum's Museum was on Park Row at that time. It was pulling in enormous crowds all day long to see the Cardiff Giant, Tom Thumb, and dozens of other wonders: people milled about from one wonder to another while a line of people on the street outside were waiting to get in. Mr. Barnum, with his never-failing sense of showmanship, saw that if he could get the crowds to move through the museum faster and out the rear exit more people in the line waiting to get in could buy tickets and get in to see his exhibits. So he had a spectacular sign painted for his rear wall "Don't fail to see the Giant Egress—right through this door." Of course when you walked through the door you found, instead of another exhibit, that you were on the street and you probably laughed at yourself and advised your friends to take in the museum, knowing that they too would probably behave in the same manner.

Hartford must have been familiar with Barnum's Museum—how could anyone in New York miss its flamboyant signs and its brass band in front? He must have spent hours studying the methods of the great showman, noting the gaily colored museum front with rows of gas lights across it and the band blaring out "Oh, Susanna!" and other tunes of the day, and the crowds loving it, because Mr. Hartford proceeded to borrow the very same techniques to sell tea.

He opened a store just across City Hall Park, a minute's walk from Barnum's Museum, and what a store it was—nothing like it had ever been seen among retail stores. Thirty-one Vesey Street was the address. Outside a huge gaslit T illuminated a store front of "real Chinese vermilion and flaked gold." And inside the walls were lined with bins gaily painted in the same colors. Japanese lanterns were everywhere and huge gaslit chandeliers dotted the ceiling over the Chinese pagoda that was to serve as the cashier's desk.

And on Saturday evenings when New Yorkers liked to go for a walk to look in the shop windows of the neighborhood, sure enough young Mr. Hartford had a real brass band out in front.

The store was a success from the very day it opened. George Hartford was smart enough to know that all this glitter and noise might attract people once, but nothing but good tea at low prices would bring them back again and again. In a couple of years he had outgrown that store and taken a larger place next door. His next step was to put in a mail-order department. He ran advertisements in some of the magazines to let the people inland know about his low prices and orders came in by the hundreds. By this time he had added coffee to the line and, shortly afterwards, extracts and flavoring materials.

In 1869, just ten years after he had opened up, an event happened out West that was to have a sensational effect on our whole economy—the joining of the West Coast to the East Coast by rail. And Mr. Hartford was quick to take every advantage of the excitement. With the whole country talking about the Atlantic and Pacific with visions of what it could mean for everyone, Mr. Hartford changed the name of the store to "The Great Atlantic & Pacific Tea Company." In his magazine advertisements he told the reader that he could now deliver fresh tea only thirty, or at most forty, days out of China instead of the four months that were necessary when ships had to go around the Horn to reach our East Coast. His next step was to open a branch store in Boston and following this another in Philadelphia. Soon they appeared in the larger cities up and down the East Coast.

Mr. Hartford had long had his eyes on the fast-growing Midwest but it seems to have taken the Chicago Fire of 1871 to stir him into action. The fire had burned out thousands of Chicago homes and many more thousands of homeless people were walking the ruined city with nothing to eat. Charitable organizations all over the country sent huge stores of food. The A&P also sent a sizable load, and within a few weeks Hartford had opened his first regular store in Chicago.

By 1880 Hartford had a total of ninety-five stores scattered from Boston west as far as Milwaukee. This year his son George, aged fifteen, went to work as cashier at 31 Vesey Street; in 1888 his second son John, aged sixteen, joined them, and soon the two boys were bearing a large part of the responsibility for a very large business.

All this time Hartford was adding more and more items to his stock, and the shops were no longer just tea and coffee stores. Now the housewife could buy at the A&P almost anything that she could get in any food store. Most items were dipped out of a barrel or box—individual packaging was far in the future. But with only about a hundred small stores (nothing like the supermarkets of today) and a population of roughly twenty-five million in the area, Hartford was still missing around 80 to 90 per cent of the possible business. Not all the customers he might have could get to his stores. Roads were too bad, hub-deep in mud in wet weather, dusty in dry. As we have noted, the road-building binge of the nineteenth century did not last long, and in the 1880's roads were actually in worse condition than in the 1830's, railroads having superseded them. For most customers a trip of even four or five miles to a store in town was a great inconvenience for the shopper. And so the Hartford family went into the business of peddling. They built a fleet of wagons designed to carry their goods, decorated them in red and gold to look like their stores, and trained an army of men to drive them into areas where there were no convenient stores. The driver of each wagon was the manager, the clerk, the cashier—and sometimes even the veterinarian or blacksmith if one was needed.

No exact figures are available on how many of these traveling stores were operated by the A&P; but they far outnumbered the stationary stores at one time. The total increased until the year 1910 when the beginning of the Motor Age made them out of date, and eventually they disappeared. But for a generation they were a familiar sight on country roads and town and village streets.

There were other traveling food peddlers up to that time too, and they must have numbered in the thousands. They are gone; but it is interesting to note that several large chain grocers now, in the 1960's, are experimenting with traveling food stores in trucks—for the convenience of families who do not have two cars. If they succeed we will have made a full circle back to the days of our ancestors. Meanwhile the heritage of the Yankee peddler remains in the form of the many thriving enterprises that were founded on the ingenuity and ambition of the young men who traveled our wilderness roads with packs on their backs.

Bibliography

BARCK, CARL, A.M., M.D. "The History of Spectacles." Lecture before the Academy of Science, St. Louis. Reprinted from *The Open Court* for April, 1907.

BUTTERFIELD, ROGER. *The American Past.* New York: Simon & Schuster, 1947.

BOSWELL, VICTOR R. "Our Vegetable Travelers," *The National Geographic Magazine,* August, 1949. Washington, D.C.: The National Geographic Society, 1949.

CARSON, GERALD. "Country Stores in Early New England," Old Sturbridge Village Booklet Series, Meriden, Connecticut: Old Sturbridge, Inc., 1955.

CLEMENS, SAMUEL L. *Life on the Mississippi* (Signet CD111). New York: The New American Library, 1961.

COLLES, CHRISTOPHER. *Roads of the U.S.A.* Cambridge, Mass.: Harvard University Press, 1961.

Colonial Williamsburg. *Official Guidebook.* Colonial Williamsburg, Inc., 1962.

CUMMINGS, HUBERTIS. "The Pennsylvania Canals." Historic Pennsylvania Leaflet No. 1. Harrisburg: Commonwealth of Pennsylvania, Pennsylvania Historical and Museum Commission, 1957.

DREPPARD, CARL W. *American Clocks and Clockmakers.* Newton Centre, Mass.: Branford.

DUNBAR, SEYMOUR. *History of Travel in America.* Indianapolis: Bobbs-Merrill Co., 1915.

DWIGHT, TIMOTHY. *Travels in New England and New York.* London: W. Baynes & Son, 1823.

EARLE, ALICE MORSE. *Stage Coach and Tavern Days*. London: Macmillan & Co., 1927.

EATON, ALLEN H. *Handicrafts of New England*. New York: Harper & Brothers Publishers, 1949.

ECKHARDT, GEORGE H. *Pennsylvania Clocks and Clockmakers: An Epic of Early American Science, Industry, and Craftsmanship*. New York: The Devin-Adair Co., 1955.

EVANS, CERINDA W. *Collis Potter Huntington*. 2 Vols. Newport News, Va.: The Mariner's Museum Publication No. 24, 1954.

FANNING, M. LEONARD. *Cyrus Hall McCormick: Father of Farm Mechanization*. (Fathers of Industries Series.) The Mercer Publishing Company.

GITTINS, BERT S. *Land of Plenty* (Second ed). Chicago: Farm Equipment Institute, 1959.

GOULD, MARY EARLE. *Early American Wooden Ware and Other Kitchen Utensils*. Springfield, Mass.: The Pond-Ekberg Co., 1948.

GRAHAM, LLOYD. *Niagara Country*. New York: Duell, Sloan & Pearce, 1949.

HATCHER, HARLAN. *The Western Reserve*. Indianapolis: Bobbs-Merrill Co., 1949.

HOLBROOK, STEWART. *The Age of the Moguls*. (Mainstream of America Series.) Garden City, N.Y.: Doubleday & Co., Inc., 1954.

HULBERT, ARCHER BUTLER. *The Historic Highways of America*. Cleveland, Ohio: A. H. Clark Co., 1905.

JACKSON, JOSEPH. *America's Most Historic Highway*. Philadelphia: John Wanamaker, 1926.

JONES, LESTER W. (ed.) *A Treasury of Spices*. New York: American Spice Trade Association, 1956.

KINZIE, JUILIETTE AUGUSTA McGILL. *Wau-Bun*. London: S. Low, Son & Co., 1856.

MACE, WILLIAM H. *American History*. Skokie, Ill.: Rand McNally, 1925.

MARLOWE, GEORGE FRANCIS. *Coaching Roads of Old New England*. New York: The Macmillan Co., 1945.

MARTI-IBÁÑEZ, FELIX, M.D. *The Epic of Medicine*. New York: Clarkson N. Potter, Inc., 1962.

MATEAUX, C. L. *The Wonderland of Work*. London: Cassell & Co., Ltd.

MATHEWS, ALFRED. *Ohio and Her Western Reserve*. New York: Appleton-Century, 1902.

BIBLIOGRAPHY

MOORE, MABEL ROBERTS. *Hitchcock Chairs*. New Haven: Published for the Tercentary Commission by the Yale University Press. Pub. no. 15, 1933.

NEVINS, ALLAN. *Times of Trial*. New York: Knopf, 1958.

NUTTING, WALLACE. *The Clock Book*. Garden City, N.Y.: Garden City Publishing Company and the Old America Company, 1935.

PALMER, BROOKS. *The Book of American Clocks*. New York: Macmillan Co., 1950.

Public Works Agency, *Highways of History*. Washington, D.C.: Public Roads Administration.

QUAIFE, M. M. *Chicago and the Old Northwest*. Chicago: Univ. of Chicago Press, 1913.

ROBINSON, NUGENT. *Collier's Cyclopedia of Commercial and Social Information*. New York: Peter Fenelon Collier Publisher, 1882.

SCULL, P. "Packroad to Yesterday." *The American Heritage Magazine*, Vol. 7, pp. 58-61. New York: The American Heritage Publishing Co., 1956.

SHEPARD, ODELL. *Connecticut, Past and Present*. London: Knopf, 1939.

SPARKS, JARED. *Life of George Washington*. Boston: Tappen and Dennet, 1843.

STEWART, GEORGE R. *U.S. 40*. Boston: Houghton Mifflin, 1953.

STRAUS, RALPH. *Coaches and Carriages*. London: M. Secher, 1912.

TODD, CHARLES BURR. *History of Redding, Connecticut*. New York: John A. Gray Press, 1880.

THORN, D. JORDAN. *Handbook of Old Pottery and Porcelain Marks*. New York: Tudor, 1947.

TRIPLETT, COL. FRANK. *Conquering the Wilderness*. Chicago: National Book and Picture Co., 1883.

TROLLOPE, FRANCES. *Domestic Manners of the Americans*. New York: Knopf, 1949.

WALLACE, PAUL A. W. "Historic Indian Paths of Pennsylvania." (Pennsylvania Historical Reprints.) Reprinted from *The Pennsylvania Magazine of History and Biography,* quarterly journal of the Historical Society of Pennsylvania, Vol. LXXVI, No. 4 (October, 1952).

WOODWARD, W. E. *The Way Our People Lived: An Intimate American History*. New York: E. P. Dutton & Co., Inc., 1944.

WRIGHT, CARROLL D. *New Century Book of Facts*. Springfield, Mass.: King Richardson Company, 1911.

Wright, Richardson. *Hawkers and Walkers in Early America.* Philadelphia: J. B. Lippincott Co., 1927.

Wyler, Seymour B. *The Book of Old Silver.* New York: Crown Publishers, Inc., 1937.